ONE FLEW OVER THE CUCKOO'S NEST

Ken Kesey

SPARK PUBLISHING

Spark Publishing
A Division of Barnes & Noble
120 Fifth Avenue
New York, NY 10011
www.sparknotes.com

ISBN-13: 978-1-4114-0713-8
ISBN-10: 1-4114-0713-X

Please submit changes or report errors to www.sparknotes.com/errors.

Printed in the United States

10 9 8 7 6 5 4 3

CONTENTS

Context

KEN KESEY WAS BORN in 1935 in La Junta, Colorado. He grew up in Oregon and returned there to teach until his death in November 2001. After being elected the boy most likely to succeed by his high school class, Kesey enrolled in the University of Oregon. He married in 1956, a year before receiving his bachelor's degree. Afterward, he won a fellowship to a creative writing program at Stanford University. While he was there, he became a volunteer in a program to test the effects of new drugs at the local Veterans Administration hospital. During this time, he discovered LSD and became interested in studying alternative methods of perception. He soon took a job in a mental institution, where he spoke extensively to the patients.

Kesey's *One Flew Over the Cuckoo's Nest* is based largely on his experiences with mental patients. Through the conflict between Nurse Ratched and Randle Patrick McMurphy, the novel explores the themes of individuality and rebellion against conformity, ideas that were widely discussed at a time when the United States was committed to opposing communism and totalitarian regimes around the world. However, Kesey's approach, directing criticism at American institutions themselves, was revolutionary in a way that would find greater expression during the sixties. The novel, published in 1962, was an immediate success.

With his newfound wealth, Kesey purchased a farm in California, where he and his friends experimented heavily with LSD. He soon became the focus of a growing drug cult. He believed that using LSD to achieve altered states of mind could improve society. Kesey's high profile as an LSD guru in the midst of the public's growing hysteria against it and other drugs attracted the attention of legal authorities. Kesey fled to Mexico after he was caught trying to flush some marijuana down a toilet. When he returned to the United States, he was arrested and sent to jail for several months.

In 1964, Kesey led a group of friends called the Merry Pranksters on a road trip across the United States in a bus named Furthur. The participants included Neil Cassady, who had also participated in the 1950s version of this trip with Jack Kerouac and company. The trip involved massive consumption of LSD and numerous subversive adventures. The exploits of the Merry Pranksters are detailed in

Tom Wolfe's *The Electric Kool-Aid Acid Test*. This book became a must-read for the hippie generation, and much of the generation's slang and philosophy comes directly from its pages.

Dale Wasserman adapted *One Flew Over the Cuckoo's Nest* into a play version that ran on Broadway in 1963, with Kirk Douglas in the leading role. In 1975, a movie version was released without Kesey's permission, directed by Milos Forman. It was extremely successful, though quite different from the novel. It was nominated for nine Academy Awards and swept the five major categories. As a result, for many people familiar with the film version, Randle Mc-Murphy will forever be associated with Jack Nicholson, the famous actor who portrayed him.

PLOT OVERVIEW

CHIEF BROMDEN, THE HALF-INDIAN NARRATOR of *One Flew Over the Cuckoo's Nest,* has been a patient in an Oregon psychiatric hospital for ten years. His paranoia is evident from the first lines of the book, and he suffers from hallucinations and delusions. Bromden's worldview is dominated by his fear of what he calls the Combine, a huge conglomeration that controls society and forces people into conformity. Bromden pretends to be deaf and dumb and tries to go unnoticed, even though he is six feet seven inches tall.

The mental patients, all male, are divided into Acutes, who can be cured, and Chronics, who cannot be cured. They are ruled by Nurse Ratched, a former army nurse who runs the ward with harsh, mechanical precision. During daily Group Meetings, she encourages the Acutes to attack each other in their most vulnerable places, shaming them into submission. If a patient rebels, he is sent to receive electroshock treatments and sometimes a lobotomy, even though both practices have fallen out of favor with the medical community.

When Randle McMurphy arrives as a transfer from the Pendleton Work Farm, Bromden senses that something is different about him. McMurphy swaggers into the ward and introduces himself as a gambling man with a zest for women and cards. After McMurphy experiences his first Group Meeting, he tells the patients that Nurse Ratched is a ball-cutter. The other patients tell him that there is no defying her, because in their eyes she is an all-powerful force. McMurphy makes a bet that he can make Ratched lose her temper within a week.

At first, the confrontations between Ratched and McMurphy provide entertainment for the other patients. McMurphy's insubordination, however, soon stimulates the rest of them into rebellion. The success of his bet hinges on a failed vote to change the television schedule to show the World Series, which is on during the time allotted for cleaning chores. McMurphy stages a protest by sitting in front of the blank television instead of doing his work, and one by one the other patients join him. Nurse Ratched loses control and screams at them. Bromden observes that an outsider would think all of them were crazy, including the nurse.

In Part II, McMurphy, flush with victory, taunts Nurse Ratched and the staff with abandon. Everyone expects him to get sent to the Disturbed ward, but Nurse Ratched keeps him in the regular ward, thinking the patients will soon see that he is just as cowardly as everyone else. McMurphy eventually learns that involuntarily committed patients are stuck in the hospital until the staff decides they are cured. When McMurphy realizes that he is at Nurse Ratched's mercy, he begins to submit to her authority. By this time, however, he has unintentionally become the leader for the other patients, and they are confused when he stops standing up for them. Cheswick, dismayed when McMurphy fails to join him in a stand against Nurse Ratched, drowns in the pool in a possible suicide.

Cheswick's death signals to McMurphy that he has unwittingly taken on the responsibility of rehabilitating the other patients. He also witnesses the harsh reality of electroshock therapy and becomes genuinely frightened by the power wielded by the staff. The weight of his obligation to the other patients and his fear for his own life begins to wear down his strength and his sanity. Nevertheless, in Part III, McMurphy arranges a fishing trip for himself and ten other patients. He shows them how to defuse the hostility of the outside world and enables them to feel powerful and masculine as they catch large fish without his help. He also arranges for Billy Bibbit to lose his virginity later in the novel, by making a date between Billy and Candy Starr, a prostitute from Portland.

Back on the ward in Part IV, McMurphy reignites the rebellion by getting into a fistfight with the aides to defend George Sorenson. Bromden joins in, and they are both sent to the Disturbed ward for electroshock therapy. McMurphy acts as if the shock treatments do not affect him, and his heroic reputation grows. Nurse Ratched brings him back to the ward so the other patients can see his weakened state. The patients urge McMurphy to escape, but he has arranged Billy's date for that night, and he refuses to let Billy down. McMurphy bribes Mr. Turkle, the night aide, to sneak Candy into the hospital, and they have a party on the ward. Billy has sex with Candy while McMurphy and the other patients smoke marijuana and drink. Harding tries to get McMurphy to escape with Candy and Sandy to Mexico, but McMurphy is too wasted and falls asleep.

The aides discover the mess the next morning, setting off a series of violent events. When Nurse Ratched finds Billy with Candy, she threatens to tell Billy's mother. Billy becomes hysterical and commits suicide by cutting his throat. McMurphy attacks Ratched, ripping open the front of her dress and attempting to strangle her. In retaliation, she has him lobotomized, and he returns to the ward as a vegetable. However, Ratched has lost her tyrannical power over the ward. The patients transfer to other wards or check themselves out of the hospital. Bromden suffocates McMurphy in his bed, enabling him to die with some dignity rather than live as a symbol of Ratched's power. Bromden, having recovered the immense strength that he had believed lost during his time in the mental ward, escapes from the hospital by breaking through a window.

CHARACTER LIST

Chief Bromden   The narrator of *One Flew Over the Cuckoo's Nest*. Chief Bromden is the son of the chief of the Columbia Indians and a white woman. He suffers from paranoia and hallucinations, has received multiple electroshock treatments, and has been in the hospital for ten years, longer than any other patient in the ward. Bromden sees modern society as a huge, oppressive conglomeration that he calls the Combine and the hospital as a place meant to fix people who do not conform. Bromden chronicles the story of the mental ward while developing his perceptual abilities and regaining a sense of himself as an individual.

Randle McMurphy   The novel's protagonist. Randle McMurphy is a big, redheaded gambler, a con man, and a backroom boxer. His body is heavily scarred and tattooed, and he has a fresh scar across the bridge of his nose. He was sentenced to six months at a prison work farm, and when he was diagnosed as a psychopath—for "too much fighting and fucking"—he did not protest because he thought the hospital would be more comfortable than the work farm. McMurphy serves as the unlikely Christ figure in the novel—the dominant force challenging the establishment and the ultimate savior of the victimized patients.

Nurse Ratched   The head of the hospital ward. Nurse Ratched, the novel's antagonist, is a middle-aged former army nurse. She rules her ward with an iron hand and masks her humanity and femininity behind a stiff, patronizing facade. She selects her staff for their submissiveness, and she weakens her patients through a psychologically manipulative program designed to destroy their self-esteem. Ratched's emasculating, mechanical ways slowly drain all traces of humanity from her patients.

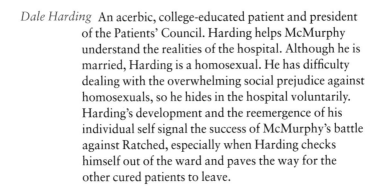

Dale Harding An acerbic, college-educated patient and president of the Patients' Council. Harding helps McMurphy understand the realities of the hospital. Although he is married, Harding is a homosexual. He has difficulty dealing with the overwhelming social prejudice against homosexuals, so he hides in the hospital voluntarily. Harding's development and the reemergence of his individual self signal the success of McMurphy's battle against Ratched, especially when Harding checks himself out of the ward and paves the way for the other cured patients to leave.

Billy Bibbit A shy patient. Billy has a bad stutter and seems much younger than his thirty-one years. Billy Bibbit is dominated by his mother, one of Nurse Ratched's close friends. Billy is voluntarily in the hospital, as he is afraid of the outside world.

Doctor Spivey A mild-mannered doctor who may be addicted to opiates. Nurse Ratched chose Doctor Spivey as the doctor for her ward because he is as easily cowed and dominated as the patients. With McMurphy's arrival, he, like the patients, begins to assert himself. He often supports McMurphy's unusual plans for the ward, such as holding a carnival.

Charles Cheswick The first patient to support McMurphy's rebellion against Nurse Ratched's power. Cheswick, a man of much talk and little action, drowns in the pool—possibly a suicide—after McMurphy does not support Cheswick when Cheswick takes a stand against Nurse Ratched. Cheswick's death is significant in that it awakens McMurphy to the extent of his influence and the mistake of his decision to conform.

Warren, Washington, Williams, and Geever Hospital aides. Warren, Washington, and Williams are Nurse Ratched's daytime aides; Geever is the nighttime aide. Nurse Ratched hired them because they are filled with hatred and will submit to her wishes completely.

Candy Starr A beautiful, carefree prostitute from Portland. Candy Starr accompanies McMurphy and the other patients on the fishing trip, and then comes to the ward for a late-night party that McMurphy arranges.

George Sorenson A hospital patient, a big Swede, and a former seaman. McMurphy recruits George Sorenson to be captain for the fishing excursion. He is nicknamed "Rub-a-Dub George" by the aides because he has an intense phobia toward dirtiness. McMurphy's defense of George leads McMurphy to his first electroshock treatment.

Pete Bancini A hospital patient who suffered brain damage when he was born. Pete Bancini continually declares that he is tired, and at one point he tells the other patients that he was born dead.

Martini Another hospital patient. Martini lives in a world of delusional hallucinations, but McMurphy includes him in the board and card games with the other patients.

Old Blastic A patient who is a vegetable. Bromden has a prophetic dream about a mechanical slaughterhouse in which Old Blastic is murdered. He wakes up to discover that Old Blastic died in the night.

Ellis A patient who was once an Acute. Ellis's excessive electroshock therapy transformed him into a Chronic. In the daytime, he is nailed to the wall. He frequently urinates on himself.

The lifeguard A patient and a former football player. The lifeguard was committed to the ward eight years ago. He often experiences hallucinations. The lifeguard reveals a key fact to McMurphy—that committed patients can leave only when Nurse Ratched permits— which changes McMurphy's initial rebelliousness into temporary conformity.

Sandy Gilfillian A prostitute who knows McMurphy.

Ruckly A Chronic patient. Ruckly, like Ellis, was once an Acute, but was transformed into a Chronic due to a botched lobotomy.

Scanlon The only Acute besides McMurphy who was involuntarily committed to the hospital. Scanlon has fantasies of blowing things up.

Sefelt and Frederickson Epileptic patients. Sefelt hates to take his medications because they make his teeth fall out, so he gives them to Frederickson, who likes to take Sefelt's dose in addition to his own. Although Sefelt and Frederickson require more medical care than some of the other nonmedicated patients, they still do not receive much care or attention by the staff, who are much more concerned with making the disorderly patients orderly.

Mr. Turkle The black nighttime orderly for Nurse Ratched's ward. Mr. Turkle is kind to Bromden, untying the sheets that confine him to his bed at night, and he goes along with the nighttime ward party.

Maxwell Taber A former patient who stayed in Nurse Ratched's ward before McMurphy arrived. When Maxwell Taber questioned the nurse's authority, she punished him with electroshock therapy. After the treatments made him completely docile, he was allowed to leave the hospital. He is considered a successful cure by the hospital staff.

Chief Tee Ah Millatoona Chief Bromden's father, also known as The Pine That Stands Tallest on the Mountain, is chief of the Columbia Indians. He married a Caucasian woman and took her last name. She made him feel small and drove him to alcoholism. The chief's marriage and submission to a white woman makes an important statement about the oppression of the natural order by modern society and also reflects white society's encroachment on Native Americans.

Public Relation   A fat, bald bureaucrat who wears a girdle. Public Relation leads tours of the ward, pointing out that it is nice and pleasant.

Nurse Pilbow   A strict Catholic with a prominent birthmark on her face that she attempts to scrub away. Nurse Pilbow is afraid of the patients' sexuality.

Rawler   A patient on the Disturbed ward. Rawler commits suicide by cutting off his testicles. This actual castration symbolizes the psychological emasculation to which the patients are routinely subjected.

ANALYSIS OF MAJOR CHARACTERS

CHIEF BROMDEN

Chief Bromden, nicknamed "Chief Broom" because the aides make him sweep the halls, narrates *One Flew Over the Cuckoo's Nest.* Although he says that he is telling the story about "the hospital, and her, and the guys—and about McMurphy," he is also telling the story of his own journey toward sanity. When the novel begins, Bromden is paranoid, bullied, and surrounded much of the time by a hallucinated fog that represents both his medicated state and his desire to hide from reality. Moreover, he believes that he is extremely weak, even though he used to be immensely strong; because he believes it, he *is* extremely weak. By the end of the novel, the fog has cleared, and Bromden has recovered the personal strength to euthanize McMurphy, escape from the hospital, and record his account of the events.

Bromden is six feet seven inches tall (or six feet eight inches, the book is inconsistent), but because he has been belittled for so long, he thinks he "used to be big, but not no more." He has been a patient in an Oregon psychiatric hospital for ten years. Everyone in the hospital believes that he is deaf and dumb. When McMurphy begins to pull him out of the fog, he realizes the source of his charade: "it wasn't me that started acting deaf; it was people that first started acting like I was too dumb to hear or see or say anything at all." As Bromden himself is demystified, so too is the truth behind what has oppressed him and hindered his recovery.

This oppression has been in place since Bromden's childhood. He is the son of Chief Tee Ah Millatoona, which means The Pine That Stands Tallest on the Mountain, and a white woman, Mary Louise Bromden, the dominant force in the couple. Chief Bromden bears his mother's last name; his father's acceptance of her name symbolizes her dominance over him. In one telling experience, when Bromden was ten years old, three government officials came to see his father about buying the tribe's land so they could build a hydroelectric dam, but Bromden was home alone. When he tried to speak to the officials, they acted as if he was not there. This experience sows the seeds for his withdrawal into himself, and initiates the outside world's treatment of him as if he were deaf and dumb. Bromden's mother joined forces with some of the members of the tribe to pressure Bromden's father to sell the land. Bromden, like his father, is a big man who comes to feel small and helpless.

The reason for Bromden's hospitalization is cloaked in ambiguity. He may have had a breakdown from witnessing the decline of his father or from the horrors of fighting in World War II. Both of these possible scenarios involve an emasculating and controlling authority—in the first case the government officials, in the second the army. These authority figures provide Bromden with fodder for his dark vision of society as an oppressive conglomeration that he calls the Combine. It is also possible that, like McMurphy, Bromden was sane when he entered the hospital but that his sanity slipped when he received what is rumored to be 200 electroshock treatments. The paranoia and hallucinations he suffers from, which center on hidden machines in the hospital that physically and psychologically control the patients, can be read as metaphors for the dehumanization he has experienced in his life.

Randle McMurphy

Randle McMurphy—big, loud, sexual, dirty, and confident—is an obvious foil for the quiet and repressed Bromden and the sterile and mechanical Nurse Ratched. His loud, free laughter stuns the other patients, who have grown accustomed to repressed emotions. Throughout the entire moment of his introduction, not a single voice rises to meet his.

McMurphy represents sexuality, freedom, and self-determination—characteristics that clash with the oppressed ward, which is controlled by Nurse Ratched. Through Chief Bromden's narration, the novel establishes that McMurphy is not, in fact, crazy, but rather that he is trying to manipulate the system to his advantage. His belief that the hospital would be more comfortable than the Pendleton Work Farm, where he was serving a six-month sentence, haunts McMurphy later when he discovers the power Nurse Ratched wields over him—that she can send him for electroshock treatments and keep him committed as long as she likes. McMurphy's sanity contrasts with what Kesey implies is an insane institution.

Whether insane or not, the hospital is undeniably in control of the fates of its patients. McMurphy's fate as the noncomforming insurrectionist is foreshadowed by the fate of Maxwell Taber, a former patient who was also, according to Nurse Ratched, a manipulator. Taber was subjected to electroshock treatments and possibly brain work, which leaves him docile and unable to think. When Ratched equates McMurphy with Taber, we get an inkling of McMurphy's prospects. McMurphy's trajectory through the novel is the opposite of Bromden's: he starts out sane and powerful but ends up a helpless vegetable, having sacrificed himself for the benefit of all the patients.

McMurphy's self-sacrifice on behalf of his ward-mates echoes Christ's sacrifice of himself on the cross to redeem humankind. McMurphy's actions frequently parallel Christ's actions in the Gospels. McMurphy undergoes a kind of baptism upon entering the ward, and he slowly gathers disciples around him as he increases his rebellion against Ratched. When he takes the group of patients fishing, he is like Christ leading his twelve disciples to the sea to test their faith. Finally, McMurphy's ultimate sacrifice, his attack on Ratched, combined with the symbolism of the cross-shaped electroshock table and McMurphy's request for "a crown of thorns," cements the image of the Christ-like martyrdom that McMurphy has achieved by sacrificing his freedom and sanity.

NURSE RATCHED

A former army nurse, Nurse Ratched represents the oppressive mechanization, dehumanization, and emasculation of modern society—in Bromden's words, the Combine. Her nickname is "Big Nurse," which sounds like Big Brother, the name used in George Orwell's novel *1984* to refer to an oppressive and all-knowing authority. Bromden describes Ratched as being like a machine, and her behavior fits this description: even her name is reminiscent of a mechanical tool, sounding like both "ratchet" and "wretched." She enters the novel, and the ward, "with a gust of cold." Ratched has complete control over every aspect of the ward, as well as almost complete control over her own emotions. In the first few pages we see her show her "hideous self" to Bromden and the aides, only to regain her doll-like composure before any of the patients catch a glimpse. Her ability to present a false self suggests that the mechanistic and oppressive forces in society gain ascendance through the dishonesty of the powerful. Without being aware of the oppression, the quiet and docile slowly become weakened and gradually are subsumed.

Nurse Ratched does possess a nonmechanical and undeniably human feature in her large bosom, which she conceals as best she can beneath a heavily starched uniform. Her large breasts both exude sexuality and emphasize her role as a twisted mother figure for the ward. She is able to act like "an angel of mercy" while at the same time shaming the patients into submission; she knows their weak spots and exactly where to peck. The patients try to please her during the Group Meetings by airing their dirtiest, darkest secrets, and then they feel deeply ashamed for how she made them act, even though they have done nothing. She maintains her power by the strategic use of shame and guilt, as well as by a determination to "divide and conquer" her patients.

McMurphy manages to ruffle Ratched because he plays her game: he picks up on her weak spots right away. He uses his overt sexuality to throw her off her machinelike track, and he is not taken in by her thin facade of compassion or her falsely therapeutic tactics. When McMurphy rips her shirt open at the end of the novel, he symbolically exposes her hypocrisy and deceit, and she is never able to regain power.

THEMES, MOTIFS & SYMBOLS

THEMES

Themes are the fundamental and often universal ideas explored in a literary work.

WOMEN AS CASTRATORS

With the exception of the prostitutes, who are portrayed as good, the women in *One Flew Over the Cuckoo's Nest* are uniformly threatening and terrifying figures. Bromden, the narrator, and Mc-Murphy, the protagonist, both tend to describe the suffering of the mental patients as a matter of emasculation or castration at the hands of Nurse Ratched and the hospital supervisor, who is also a woman. The fear of women is one of the novel's most central features. The male characters seem to agree with Harding, who complains, "We are victims of a matriarchy here."

Indeed, most of the male patients have been damaged by relationships with overpowering women. For instance, Bromden's mother is portrayed as a castrating woman; her husband took her last name, and she turned a big, strong chief into a small, weak alcoholic. According to Bromden, she built herself up emotionally, becoming bigger than either he or his father, by constantly putting them down. Similarly, Billy Bibbit's mother treats him like an infant and does not allow him to develop sexually. Through sex with Candy, Billy briefly regains his confidence. It is no coincidence that this act, which symbolically resurrects his manhood, also literally introduces his penis to sexual activity. Thus, his manhood—in both senses—returns until Ratched takes it away by threatening to tell his mother and driving him to commit suicide.

More explicit images of and references to castration appear later in the novel, cementing Kesey's idea of emasculation by the frigid nurse. When Rawler, a patient in the Disturbed ward, commits suicide by cutting off his own testicles, Bromden remarks that "all the guy had to do was wait," implying that the institution itself would have castrated him in the long run. The hospital, run by women, treats only male patients, showing how women have the ability to emasculate even the most masculine of men. Finally, near the end of the novel, after McMurphy has already received three shock treatments that do not seem to have had an effect on him, Nurse Ratched suggests taking more drastic measures: "an operation." She means, of course, a lobotomy, but McMurphy beats her to the punch by joking about castration. Both operations remove a man's individuality, freedom, and ability for sexual expression. Kesey portrays the two operations as symbolically the same.

Society's Destruction of Natural Impulses

Kesey uses mechanical imagery to represent modern society and biological imagery to represent nature. By means of mechanisms and machines, society gains control of and suppresses individuality and natural impulses. The hospital, representative of society at large, is decidedly unnatural: the aides and Nurse Ratched are described as being made of motley machine parts. In Chief Bromden's dream, when Blastic is disemboweled, rust, not blood, spills out, revealing that the hospital destroyed not only his life but his humanity as well. Bromden's realization that the hospital treats human beings in an unnatural fashion, and his concomitant growing self-awareness, occur as a surrounding fog dissipates. It is no surprise that Bromden believes this fog is a construction of machines controlled by the hospital and by Nurse Ratched.

Bromden, as the son of an Indian chief, is a combination of pure, natural individuality and a spirit almost completely subverted by mechanized society. Early on, he had free will, and he can remember and describe going hunting in the woods with his relatives and the way they spear salmon. The government, however, eventually succeeds in paying off the tribe so their fishing area can be converted into a profitable hydroelectric dam. The tribe members are banished into the technological workforce, where they become "hypnotized by routine," like the "half-life things" that Bromden witnesses coming out of the train while he is on fishing excursions. In the novel's present time, Bromden himself ends up semi-catatonic and paranoid, a mechanical drone who is still able to think and conjecture to some extent on his own.

McMurphy represents unbridled individuality and free expression—both intellectual and sexual. One idea presented in this novel is that a man's virility is equated with a state of nature, and the state of civilized society requires that he be desexualized. But McMurphy battles against letting the oppressive society make him into a machinelike drone, and he manages to maintain his individuality until his ultimate objective—bringing this individuality to the others—is complete. However, when his wildness is provoked one too many times by Nurse Ratched, he ends up being destroyed by modern society's machines of oppression.

THE IMPORTANCE OF EXPRESSING SEXUALITY

It is implied throughout the novel that a healthy expression of sexuality is a key component of sanity, and that repression of sexuality leads directly to insanity. Most of the patients have warped sexual identities because of damaging relationships with women. Perverted sexual expressions are said to take place in the ward: the aides supposedly engage in illicit "sex acts" that nobody witnesses, and on several occasions it is suggested that they rape patients, such as Taber, with Ratched's implicit permission, symbolized by the jar of Vaseline she leaves with them. Add to that the castrating power of Nurse Ratched, and the ward is left with, as Harding says, "comical little creatures who can't even achieve masculinity in the rabbit world." Missing from the halls of the mental hospital are healthy, natural expressions of sexuality between two people.

McMurphy's bold assertion of his sexuality, symbolized from the start by his playing cards depicting fifty-two sexual positions, his pride in having had a voracious fifteen-year-old lover, and his Moby-Dick boxer shorts, clashes with the sterile and sexless ward that Nurse Ratched tries to maintain. We learn that McMurphy first had sex at age ten with a girl perhaps even younger, and that her dress from that momentous occasion, which inspired him to become a "dedicated lover," still hangs outdoors for everyone to see. McMurphy's refusal to conform to society mirrors his refusal to desexualize himself, and the sexuality exuding from his personality is like a dress waving in the wind like a flag.

McMurphy attempts to cure Billy Bibbit of his stutter by arranging for him to lose his virginity with Candy. Instead, Billy gets shamed into suicide by the puritanical Ratched. By the end of the novel, McMurphy has been beaten into the ground to the point that he resorts to sexual violence—which had never been a part of his persona previous to being committed, despite Nurse Pilbow's fears—by ripping open Ratched's uniform.

FALSE DIAGNOSES OF INSANITY

McMurphy's sanity, symbolized by his free laughter, open sexuality, strength, size, and confidence, stands in contrast to what Kesey

THEMES

implies, ironically and tragically, is an insane institution. Nurse Ratched tells another nurse that McMurphy seems to be a manipulator, just like a former patient, Maxwell Taber. Taber, Bromden explains, was a "big, griping Acute" who once asked a nurse what kind of medication he was being given. He was subjected to electroshock treatments and possibly brain work, which left him docile and unable to think. The insanity of the institution is foregrounded when a man who asks a simple question is tortured and rendered inhuman. It is a Catch-22: only a sane man would question an irrational system, but the act of questioning means his sanity will inevitably be compromised.

Throughout the novel, the sane actions of men contrast with the insane actions of the institution. At the end of Part II, when McMurphy and the patients stage a protest against Nurse Ratched for not letting them watch the World Series, a sensible request for which McMurphy generates a sensible solution, she loses control and, as Bromden notes, looks as crazy as they do. Moreover, Kesey encourages the reader to consider the value of alternative states of perception, which some people also might consider crazy. For instance, Bromden's hallucinations about hidden machinery may seem crazy, but in actuality they reveal his insight into the hospital's insidious power over the patients.

In addition, when the patients go on the fishing excursion they discover that mental illness can have an aspect of power in that they can intimidate the station attendants with their insanity. Harding gives Hitler as an example in discussing Ratched, suggesting that she, like Hitler, is a psychopath who has discovered how to use her insanity to her advantage. Bromden, at one point, thinks to himself, "You're making sense, old man, a sense of your own. You're not crazy the way they think." "[C]razy the way they think," however, is all that matters in this hospital. The authority figures decide who is sane and who is insane, and by deciding it, they make it reality.

MOTIFS

Motifs are recurring structures, contrasts, and literary devices that can help to develop and inform the text's major themes.

INVISIBILITY

Many important elements in the novel are either hidden from view or invisible. For example, Bromden tries to be as invisible as possible. He has achieved this invisibility by pretending not to understand what is going on around him, so people notice him less and less. Moreover, he imagines a fog surrounding him that hides him and keeps him safe. He keeps both his body and his mind hidden.

Bromden's hallucinations about hidden machines that control the patients call attention to the fact that the power over the patients is usually covert. He imagines that the patients are implanted with tiny machines that record and control their movements from the inside. The truth is that Nurse Ratched manages to rule by insinuation, without ever having to be explicit about her accusations and threats, so it seems as though the patients themselves have absorbed her influence—she becomes a sort of twisted conscience.

When McMurphy smashes through the glass window of the Nurses' Station, his excuse is that the glass was so clean he could not see it. By smashing it, he reminds the patients that although they cannot always see Ratched's or society's manipulation, it still operates on them.

THE POWER OF LAUGHTER

The power of laughter resonates throughout the novel. McMurphy's laughter is the first genuine laughter heard on the ward in years. McMurphy's first inkling that things are strange among the patients is that none of them are able to laugh; they can only smile and snicker behind their hands. Bromden remembers a scene from his childhood when his father and relatives mocked some government officials, and he realizes how powerful their laughter was: "I forget sometimes what laughter can do." For McMurphy, laughter is a potent defense against society's insanity, and anyone who cannot laugh properly has no chance of surviving. By the end of the fishing trip, Harding, Scanlon, Doctor Spivey, and Sefelt are all finally able to participate in real, thunderous laughter, a sign of their physical and psychological recovery.

REAL VERSUS IMAGINED SIZE

Bromden describes people by their true size, not merely their physical size. Kesey implies that when people allow others, such as governments and institutions, to define their worth, they can end up far from their natural state. Nurse Ratched's true size, for example, is "big as a tractor," because she is powerful and unstoppable. Bromden, though he is six feet seven inches tall, feels much smaller and weaker. He tells McMurphy, "I used to be big, but not no more." As for McMurphy, Bromden says he is "broad as Papa was tall," and his father was named The Pine That Stands Tallest on the Mountain. Bromden says his mother was twice the size of he and his father put together, because she belittled them both so much. With McMurphy's help, Bromden is gradually "blown back up to full size" as he regains his self-esteem, sexuality, and individuality.

SYMBOLS

Symbols are objects, characters, figures, and colors used to represent abstract ideas or concepts.

THE FOG MACHINE

Fog is a phenomenon that clouds our vision of the world. In this novel, fogs symbolize a lack of insight and an escape from reality. When Bromden starts to slip away from reality, because of his medication or out of fear, he hallucinates fog drifting into the ward. He imagines that there are hidden fog machines in the vents and that they are controlled by the staff. Although it can be frightening at times, Bromden considers the fog to be a safe place; he can hide in it and ignore reality. Beyond what it means for Bromden, the fog represents the state of mind that Ratched imposes on the patients with her strict, mind-numbing routines and humiliating treatment. When McMurphy arrives, he drags all the patients out of the fog.

MCMURPHY'S BOXER SHORTS

McMurphy's boxer shorts are black satin with a pattern of white whales with red eyes. A literature major gave them to him, saying that McMurphy is himself a symbol. The shorts, of course, are also highly symbolic. First, the white whales call to mind Moby-Dick, one of the most potent symbols in American literature. One common interpretation of Moby-Dick is that the whale is a phallic symbol, which obviously suggests McMurphy's blatant sexuality—the little white whales cover McMurphy's underwear, which he gleefully reveals to Nurse Ratched. Moby-Dick also represents the pervasive evil that inspires Ahab's obsessive, futile pursuit. Here, the implication is that McMurphy is to Ratched as Moby-Dick is to Ahab. A third interpretation is that Moby-Dick stands for the power of nature, signifying McMurphy's untamed nature that conflicts with the controlled institution. Also, in Melville's novel Moby-Dick is associated with God, which resonates with McMurphy's role as a Christ figure. Finally, the whale boxer shorts poke fun at academia and its elaborate interpretations of symbols.

THE ELECTROSHOCK THERAPY TABLE

The electroshock therapy table is explicitly associated with crucifixion. It is shaped like a cross, with straps across the wrists and over the head. Moreover, the table performs a function similar to the public crucifixions of Roman times. Ellis, Ruckly, and Taber—Acutes whose lives were destroyed by electroshock therapy—serve as public examples of what happens to those who rebel against the ruling powers. Ellis makes the reference explicit: he is actually nailed to the wall. This foreshadows that McMurphy, who is associated with Christ images, will be sacrificed.

Summary & Analysis

Part I

From the beginning of the novel to McMurphy's bet with the patients

Summary

> *It's still hard for me to have a clear mind thinking on it.*
> *But it's the truth even if it didn't happen.*
> (See QUOTATIONS, p. 43)

Chief Bromden, a long-term patient in Nurse Ratched's psychiatric ward, narrates the events of the novel. The book begins as he awakens to a typical day on the ward, feeling paranoid about the illicit nighttime activities of the ward's three black aides. The aides mock him for being a pushover, even though he is six feet seven inches tall, and they make him sweep the hallways for them, nicknaming him "Chief Broom." Bromden is half Indian and pretends to be deaf and dumb; as a result, he overhears all the secrets on the ward and is barely noticed by anyone despite his stature.

Nurse Ratched, whom Bromden refers to as "the Big Nurse," enters the ward with a gust of cold air. Bromden describes Ratched as having "skin like flesh-colored enamel" and lips and fingertips the strange orange color of polished steel. Her one feminine feature is her oversized bosom, which she tries to conceal beneath a starched white uniform. When she gets angry with the aides, Bromden sees her get "big as a tractor." She orders the aides to shave Bromden, and he begins to scream and hallucinate that he is being surrounded by machine-made fog until he is forcedly medicated. He tells us that his forthcoming story about the hospital might seem "too awful to be the truth."

Bromden regains consciousness in the day room. Here, he tells us that a public relations man sometimes leads tours around the ward, pointing out the cheery atmosphere and claiming that the ward is run without the brutality exercised in previous generations. Today, the ward's monotony is interrupted when Randle McMurphy, a new patient, arrives. McMurphy's appearance is preceded by his boisterous, brassy voice and his confident, iron-heeled walk. McMurphy

laughs when the patients are stunned silent by his entrance. It is the first real laugh that the ward has heard in years.

McMurphy, a large redhead with a devilish grin, swaggers around the ward in his motorcycle cap and dirty work-farm clothes, with a leather jacket over one arm. He introduces himself as a gambling fool, saying that he requested to be transferred to the hospital to escape the drudgery of the Pendleton Work Farm. He asks to meet the "bull goose loony" so he can take over as the man in charge. He encounters Billy Bibbit, a thirty-one-year-old baby-faced man with a severe stutter, and Dale Harding, the effeminate and educated president of the Patients' Council. All the while, McMurphy sidesteps the attempts of the daytime aides to herd him into the admission routine of a shower, an injection, and a rectal thermometer.

McMurphy surveys the day room. The patients are divided into two main categories: the Acutes, who are considered curable, and the Chronics, whom Bromden, himself a Chronic, calls "machines with flaws inside that can't be repaired." The Chronics who can move around are Walkers, and the rest are either Wheelers or Vegetables. Some Chronics are patients who arrived at the hospital as Acutes but were mentally crippled by excessive shock treatment or brain surgery, common practices in the hospital. Nurse Ratched encourages the Acutes to spy on one another. If one reveals an embarrassing or incriminating personal detail, the rest race to write it in the logbook. Their reward for such disclosures is sleeping late the next morning.

Nurse Ratched runs her ward on a strict schedule, controlling every movement with absolute precision. The nurse has selected her aides for their inherent cruelty and her staff for their submissiveness. Bromden recalls Maxwell Taber, a patient who demanded information about his medications. He was sent for multiple electroshock treatments and rendered completely docile. Eventually, he was considered cured and was discharged. Bromden conceives of society as a huge, oppressive conglomeration that he calls the Combine, and he sees the hospital as a factory for "fixing up mistakes made in the neighborhoods and in the schools and in the churches."

During the Group Meeting, Nurse Ratched reopens the topic of Harding's difficult relationship with his wife. When McMurphy makes lewd jokes at the nurse's expense, she retaliates by reading his file aloud, focusing on his arrest for statutory rape. McMurphy regales the group with stories about the sexual appetite of his fifteen-year-old lover. Even Doctor Spivey enjoys McMurphy's humorous rebellion against Ratched. The doctor reads from the file, "Don't overlook the possibility that this man might be feigning psychosis to escape the drudgery of the work farm," to which McMurphy responds, "Doctor, do I look like a sane man?" McMurphy has similar defiant retorts for almost any action Ratched can consider, which perturbs Ratched greatly. McMurphy is disconcerted that the patients and the doctor can smile but not laugh. Bromden remembers a meeting that was broken up when Pete Bancini, a lifelong Chronic who constantly declared he was tired, became lucid for a moment and hit one of the aides. The nurse injected him with a sedative as he had a nervous breakdown.

During the meeting, the patients tear into Harding's sexual problems. Afterward, they are embarrassed, as always, at their viciousness. As a new participant and observer, McMurphy tells Harding that the meeting was a "pecking party"—the men acted like a bunch of chickens pecking at another chicken's wound. He warns them that a pecking party can wipe out the whole flock. When McMurphy points out that Nurse Ratched pecks first, Harding becomes defensive and states that Ratched's procedure is therapeutic. McMurphy replies that she is merely a "ball-cutter."

Harding finally agrees that Ratched is a cruel, vicious woman. He explains that everyone in the ward is a rabbit in a world ruled by wolves. They are in the hospital because they are unable to accept their roles as rabbits. Nurse Ratched is one of the wolves, and she is there to train them to accept their rabbit roles. She can make a patient shrink with shame and fear while acting like a concerned angel of mercy. Ratched never accuses directly, but she rules others through insinuation. McMurphy says that they should tell her to go to hell with her insinuating questions. Harding warns that such hostile behavior will earn a man electroshock therapy and a stay in the Disturbed ward. He points to Bromden, calling him "a six-foot-eight sweeping machine" as a result of all the shock treatment he has received. Harding asserts that the only power men have over women is sexual violence, but they cannot even exercise that power against the icy, impregnable nurse. McMurphy makes a bet with the other patients that he can make Nurse Ratched lose her temper within a week. He explains that he conned his way out of the work farm by feigning insanity, and Nurse Ratched is unprepared for an enemy with a "trigger-quick mind" like his.

Analysis

Chief Bromden, the narrator of *One Flew Over the Cuckoo's Nest,* is a complex character whose own story is revealed as he tells the story of the ward at large. Because he feigns deafness, he is privy to information that is kept from the other patients. In this way, he is a more informed narrator than any other patient. However, Bromden's reliability as a narrator is unclear because we constantly see reminders of his psychological disorder. The main indications of his illness are paranoia and frequent hallucinations. His paranoia is often justified, as the patients are indeed treated barbarically. But his hallucinations, though they seem crazy at first, metaphorically reveal his deep, intuitive understanding of his surroundings. For example, the fog machine he hallucinates represents his state of mind—he is overmedicated or simply too fearful to face the stark reality beyond the fog. The fog machine also represents the powerlessness of the patients, who are encouraged and sometimes forced by the staff to stay hidden in their own individual fogs.

Bromden sees modern society as a machinelike, oppressive force, and the hospital as a repair shop for the people who do not fit into their role as cogs in the machine. Bromden's way of interpreting the world emphasizes the oppressive social pressure to conform: those who do not conform to society's rules and conventions are considered defective products and are labeled mentally ill and sent for treatment. Thus, the mental hospital is a metaphor for the oppression Kesey sees in modern society, preceding the emergence of the 1960s counterculture. A hospital, normally a place where the ill go to be cured, becomes a dangerous place; Ellis, Ruckly, and Taber, for instance, are electroshocked until they become docile or even vegetables. The hospital is not about healing, but about dehumanizing and manipulating the patients until they are weak and willing to conform.

At the center of this controlled universe is Nurse Ratched, a representative of what Bromden calls the Combine, meaning the oppressive force of society and authority. Bromden describes her in mechanical, inhuman terms. She tries to conceal her large breasts as much as possible, and her face is like that of a doll, with a subtle edge of cruelty. Bromden imagines that the hospital is full of hidden machinery—wires, magnets, and more sinister contraptions—used by Nurse Ratched to control the patients. The nurse is, in fact, in complete control of the ward, and the tools she uses—psychological intimidation, divide-and-conquer techniques, and physical abuse—are every bit as powerful and insidious as the hidden machinery Bromden imagines.

Immediately upon his arrival, McMurphy challenges the ward with his exuberant vitality and sexuality, which are directly opposed to the sterile, mechanical nature of the hospital and modern society. He is set up as an obvious foil to Nurse Ratched, as well as to the silent and repressed Bromden. McMurphy's discussion with Harding reveals the misogynistic undertones of *One Flew Over the Cuckoo's Nest*. The patients associate matriarchy with castration, explaining the lifelessness and oppressiveness of modern society as a product of female dominance.

PART I, CONTINUED

From Bromden's description of the speeding clock to the end of Part I

SUMMARY

Bromden believes that Nurse Ratched can set the clock to any speed. Sometimes everything is painfully fast and sometimes painfully slow. His only escape is being in the fog where time does not exist. He notes that whoever controls the fog machine has not turned it on as much since McMurphy's arrival. Later, Bromden explains his captivation with McMurphy's con-artistry, which he displays while playing cards with the other patients. McMurphy wins hundreds of cigarettes and then allows his opponents to win them back. That night, McMurphy whispers to Bromden and implies that he knows he is not really deaf. Bromden does not take his night medication and has a nightmare that the hospital is a mechanical slaughterhouse. The staff hangs Old Blastic on a meat hook and slashes him open, and ash and rust pour out of the wound. Mr. Turkle wakes him from the nightmare.

Everyone wakes to McMurphy's boisterous singing in the latrine. When Williams, one of the aides, will not let him have toothpaste before the appointed time, McMurphy brushes his teeth with soap. Bromden hides his smile, as he is reminded of how his father also used to win confrontations with humor. Ratched prepares to reprimand McMurphy for his singing, but he stops her cold by stepping out of the bathroom wearing only a towel. He says that someone has taken his clothes, so he has nothing to wear. Ratched furiously reprimands the aides for failing to issue a patient's outfit to McMurphy. When

Washington, another aide, offers McMurphy an outfit, McMurphy removes the towel, revealing that all along he was wearing a pair of boxer shorts—black satin covered with white whales. Ratched manages to regain her composure with serious effort.

McMurphy is even more confident that morning. He asks Ratched to turn down the recorded music playing in the ward. She politely refuses, explaining that some of the Chronics are hard of hearing and cannot entertain themselves without the music turned up loudly. She also refuses to allow them to play cards in another room, citing a lack of staff to supervise two rooms. Doctor Spivey comes to get McMurphy for an interview, and they return talking and laughing together. At the Group Meeting, the doctor announces McMurphy's plan for the radio to be played at a higher volume, so that the hard-of-hearing patients can enjoy it more. He proposes that the other patients go to another room to read or play cards. Since the Chronics are easy to supervise, the staff can be split between the rooms. Ratched restrains herself from losing her temper.

McMurphy starts a Monopoly game with Cheswick, Martini, and Harding that goes on for three days. McMurphy makes sure he does not lose his temper with any of the staff. Once, he does get angry with the patients for being "too chicken-shit." He then requests that Ratched allow them to watch the World Series, even though it is not the regulation TV time. In order to make up for this, he proposes that they do the cleaning chores at night and watch the TV in the afternoon, but Ratched refuses to change the schedule. He proposes a vote at the Group Meeting, but only Cheswick is brave enough—or crazy enough—to defy Ratched, since the others are afraid of long-term repercussions. McMurphy, furious, says he is going to escape, and Fredrickson goads him into showing them how he would do it. McMurphy bets them that he can lift the cement control panel in the tub room and use it to break through the reinforced windows. Everybody knows it will be impossible to lift the massive panel, but he makes such a sincere effort that for one moment they all believe it is possible.

Bromden remembers how at the old hospital they did not have pictures on the wall or television. He recalls Public Relations saying, "A man that would want to run away from a place as nice as this, why, there'd be something wrong with him." Bromden senses that the fog machine has been turned on again. He explains how the fog makes him feel safe and that McMurphy keeps trying to drag them out of the fog where they will be "easy to get at." He then overhears someone talking about Old Rawler, a patient in the Disturbed unit who killed himself by cutting off his testicles. Bromden then further describes getting lost in the fog and finding himself two or three times a month at the electroshock room.

At the next Group Meeting, Bromden feels immersed in fog and cannot follow the group as they grill Billy about his stutter and failed relationship with a girl. McMurphy proposes another vote regarding the TV, with the support of some of the other patients. It is the first day of the World Series. Bromden observes the hands go up as McMurphy drags all twenty Acutes out of the fog. Ratched declares the proposal defeated, however, because none of the twenty Chronics raised their hands and McMurphy needs a majority. McMurphy finally persuades Bromden to raise his hand, but Ratched says the vote is closed. During the afternoon cleaning chores, McMurphy declares that it is time for the game. When he turns on the TV, Ratched cuts its power, but McMurphy does not budge from the armchair. The Acutes follow suit and sit in front of the blank TV. She screams and rants at them for breaking the schedule, and McMurphy wins his bet that he could make her lose her composure.

ANALYSIS

Bromden's reliability as a narrator becomes clear as we realize how incredibly observant he is. Unlike the other patients, Bromden notices how carefully McMurphy sets them up to lose their cigarettes. Moreover, Bromden's bizarre dream about Old Blastic turns out to be prophetic, demonstrating that his altered states of perception are significant rather than simply crazy. Bromden perceives the hospital not as a place promoting health but as a mechanized slaughterhouse where not only humans, but also humanity, is murdered. Old Blastic is hung on a meat hook and disemboweled, but rust and ash pour from his wound rather than flesh and blood. Bromden's dreams metaphorically reveal his profound insight into the dehumanizing and mechanizing forces of the hospital.

Bromden's hallucination that he is surrounded by fog extends to the other patients—he thinks that they are lost in fog too. This is clearly a delusion, but metaphorically it is true. The status quo enforced by Nurse Ratched functions to dull the patients' senses. Her tight routine makes everything seem to move either too slow or too fast. The too-loud music makes conversation difficult and frustrating. In response to the ever-extending fog, or a clouding of one's unique thoughts and needs, Bromden describes McMurphy's actions as dragging the patients out of the fog. By resisting Ratched, McMurphy awakens the patients to their own ability to resist her, and thereby helps them see beyond the fog. Bromden at first does not attribute his rebellious vote to his own willpower, but rather to some mysterious power on McMurphy's part. Then he later realizes, "No. That's not the truth. I lifted [my hand] myself." Bromden is very slowly beginning to see himself as an individual with free will; his recognition that the fog blankets the entire ward is an ironic indication that his own fog is beginning to lift.

McMurphy's small but continual infractions of the rules are assertions of his own individuality. McMurphy's defiance encourages the other patients to defy Ratched by gambling for cigarettes. He succeeds in drawing the other patients into rebellion against Ratched's authority, because she forbids gambling for anything but matches. Furthermore, the incident with the towel reflects McMurphy's faith in humor as a means to resist Ratched's authority. Earlier, when McMurphy suggests that the patients laugh at Ratched, Harding scoffs at the idea. Harding asserts that the only effective tool of resistance against Ratched is the penis, the instrument of male violence against dominant femininity. Although McMurphy's resistance to Ratched's authority does include a sexual element, McMurphy combines sexuality with humor, not violence. The symbolism of the encounter is heightened by McMurphy's boxers, a gift from a college student who said that McMurphy was himself a literary symbol. White whales evoke the famous Moby-Dick, a beast associated in Herman Melville's novel *Moby-Dick* with a variety of symbolic meanings, including masculinity, unseen power, insanity, and freedom. When McMurphy flaunts these symbolic boxers before Nurse Ratched, he is connected to each of these interpretations, reminding the reader that he serves as a prominent symbol within the novel.

McMurphy's display of his whale boxer shorts affirms his belief that men should not be ashamed of their sexuality, whereas making the patients ashamed of their sexuality is one of Ratched's major ways of dominating them. Ratched's strategy is evident in her treatment of Billy Bibbit, a thirty-one-year-old virgin dominated into celibacy by his mother. Though it is obvious to us that Billy needs to find a way out from under his mother's shadow, Ratched does the opposite of helping him do this, defining his sexuality in terms of inadequacy and shame. Rather than attempting to cure the patients of their problems, Ratched increases their discomfort as a way of building her own power.

McMurphy's personal rebellion against Ratched's authority expands and becomes the patients' collective rebellion, with McMurphy as their unofficial leader. When McMurphy wins his bet, he does so with the other patients' help as they all join him in protest. Meanwhile, Bromden's perceptions of the situation develop and change. When Ratched begins screaming hysterically, Bromden states that anyone who walked into the room at the moment would think they were all crazy. Insanity is no longer a characteristic of the patients alone. Before, Bromden saw the patients as defective. Now, with the help of a unified force against the mechanistic Combine, he is beginning to see the established order as defective as well.

PART II

SUMMARY
The tables are turned in the ward as everyone watches Ratched in the glassed-in Nurses' Station after her outburst. She cannot escape the patients' stares, just as they can never escape hers. Ratched strains to regain composure for the staff meeting she called. Bromden says the fog is completely gone now. He always cleans the staff room during meetings, but after his vote, he fears that everyone will realize that he is not really deaf. He goes anyway, knowing that Ratched is suspicious of him. Doctor Spivey attempts to get the meeting started while Ratched uses silence to assert her power. The staff, misreading Ratched's silence as approval, decides that McMurphy is potentially violent and should be sent to the Disturbed ward. Ratched disagrees; she declares instead that McMurphy is an ordinary man, subject to the same fears and timidity as the others. Since McMurphy is committed, Ratched knows she can control how long he spends in the hospital, and she decides to take her time with him.

Ratched assigns McMurphy the chore of cleaning the latrines, but he continues to nettle her in every way possible. Bromden marvels that the Combine has not broken him. One night, he wakes up and looks out the window and gazes in wonder at the countryside. Bromden observes a dog sniffing around the building and a flock of geese flying overhead. He watches as the dog runs toward the highway, where the headlights of an oncoming car are visible. During the Group Meetings, the patients begin to air their long-silent complaints about the rules.

The ward is taken to the hospital's pool to swim. McMurphy learns from the patient serving as the lifeguard that someone who is committed to the hospital is released only at the discretion of the staff. McMurphy had believed he could leave as soon as he served the time remaining on his work farm sentence. Cowed by his new knowledge, he behaves more conservatively around Ratched. During the next Group Meeting, Cheswick brings up the problem of cigarette rationing, but McMurphy does not support him. Ratched sends Cheswick to Disturbed for a while. After he returns, on the way to the pool, Cheswick tells McMurphy that he understands why McMurphy no longer rebels against Ratched. That day, Cheswick's fingers get stuck in the pool's drain and he drowns in what is possibly a suicide.

Sefelt, who has epilepsy, has a seizure on the floor. Fredrickson, also an epileptic, always takes Sefelt's medication. Ratched takes the opportunity to demonstrate the importance of following her advice and not "acting foolish." McMurphy, who has never seen an epileptic seizure, is very disturbed by the whole scenario. Bromden notes that McMurphy is beginning to get a "haggard, puzzled look of pressure" on his face.

Harding's wife comes for a brief visit. Harding mocks her poor grammar, and she says she wishes his limp-wristed friends would stop coming to their house to ask about him. After she leaves, McMurphy angrily erupts when Harding asks for his opinion of her, saying, "I've got worries of my own without getting hooked with yours. So just quit!" The patients are then taken to get chest X rays for TB, and McMurphy learns that Ratched can send anyone she wants for electroshock therapy and even a lobotomy in some cases, despite the fact that both practices are outdated. McMurphy tells the other patients that he knows now why they encouraged his rebellion without informing him about the consequences. He now understands that they submit to her not only because she is able to authorize these treatments, but also because she determines when they can leave the hospital. Harding informs him that, to the contrary, Scanlon is the only Acute aside from McMurphy who is committed. The rest of the Acutes are in the hospital voluntarily and could leave whenever they chose. McMurphy, completely perplexed, asks Billy Bibbit why he chooses to stay when he could be outside driving a convertible and romancing pretty girls. Billy Bibbit begins to cry and shouts that he and the others are not as big, strong, and brave as McMurphy.

McMurphy buys three cartons of cigarettes at the canteen. After the Group Meeting, Ratched announces that she and Doctor Spivey think the patients should be punished for their insubordination against the cleaning schedule a few weeks before. Since they did not apologize or show any remorse, she and Spivey have decided to take away the second game room. Everyone, including the Chronics, turns to see how McMurphy reacts. McMurphy smiles and tips his hat. Ratched thinks that she has regained control, but, after the meeting, McMurphy calmly walks to the glass-enclosed Nurses' Station where she is sitting. He says that he wants some of his cigarettes and punches his hand through the glass. He claims that the glass was so spotless that he forgot it was even there.

ANALYSIS

The staff meeting illustrates the unbelievable extent of Nurse Ratched's power in the hospital, even in the face of disruptions by a clever, sharp-witted patient like McMurphy. After McMurphy learns of her true power—her responsibility for his release and her ability to administer inhumane treatments—no one dares deny her authority even after her hysterical fit. She quickly reconsolidates her power over the staff before they can doubt her. Ratched's actions indicate her clear-thinking, premeditated approach to dealing with McMurphy. She chooses to keep McMurphy on the ward to prevent him from attaining the status of a martyr. Moreover, she realizes that sending him off the ward would be tantamount to declaring defeat. Ratched would rather confront McMurphy directly. She is comforted to know that she has complete control over his future, and that once he realizes it too, he will not dare to disobey her.

Up to this point, McMurphy's rebellions have largely been self-motivated, although they have ended up benefiting others as well. Now the other men are discovering their own individual desires and begin to follow his lead: Cheswick demands that the rationing of cigarettes be ended, and Bromden stops taking his sleeping pill. Bromden's transformation from a pretend deaf-mute into a man who can think for himself results from his observation and admiration of McMurphy. Although Bromden is physically much larger than McMurphy, he sees himself as weak and small, and he marvels at McMurphy's strength. He realizes that McMurphy's power comes from his ability to "be who he is," to maintain his individuality within the Combine's institutions. With this new knowledge, Bromden and the other patients slowly resurrect their suppressed individuality.

Bromden's realization, upon looking out the window, that the hospital is in the countryside symbolizes the broadening of his perceptual abilities under McMurphy's influence. He watches as animals interact with man-made creations. This scene of nature versus machine echoes the situation occurring within the hospital's walls. The geese belong entirely to the wild, undomesticated world. The car represents the oppressive, mechanized modern society. The dog, as a domesticated creature, is situated in between. Bromden notes that the dog and the car are headed for "the same spot of pavement." The implication is that the dog will run into the car and be killed by the overwhelmingly larger machine. This image signifies that when one tries to defy modern society's mechanized, conventional imperatives, one runs the risk of experiencing annihilation rather than victory.

After McMurphy learns that Ratched will determine when he can leave the hospital, he chooses to conform to the hospital's set of norms and rules. McMurphy doesn't yet understand the responsibility that he has assumed by serving as the ward's most effective teacher of resistance. This responsibility becomes apparent when Cheswick dies. McMurphy realizes that by ending his rebellion and conforming to Ratched's ways to save himself, he has become complicit with the destructive Combine.

The knowledge of his own complacency with the Combine strikes McMurphy strongly and influences him to resume his rebellion, although with a new sense of the ramifications of rebellion. He now acts with the full knowledge of his situation and the punishments that Ratched may inflict on him in response to his continued opposition. He now knowingly assumes the role of leader that he naively assumed earlier. Rather than being a selfish action, his resumed rebellion is calculated to benefit the other patients. In addition, McMurphy no longer relies on humorous nettling as his weapon in this rebellion. McMurphy's strength becomes less mental and more corporeal. Breaking the window is his first act of violence—far more serious than his humorous jabs. Moreover, the glass, which is kept so spotless that it is almost invisible, represents the control Nurse Ratched has over the patients; it is so deviously subtle that they sometimes forget it is there. By breaking the glass, McMurphy reminds the other patients that her power over them is always present, while simultaneously suggesting that their knowledge of her power renders that power breakable.

PART III

SUMMARY

After breaking the glass at the Nurses' Station, McMurphy is back to his old troublemaking ways. Even Doctor Spivey begins to assert himself with the nurse. The aides put a piece of cardboard where McMurphy broke the glass, and Ratched continues to sit behind it as if it were transparent—she looks like "a picture turned to the wall." Ratched rejects McMurphy's petition for an Accompanied Pass, which is a permission to spend time outside the ward while attended by another person. McMurphy wants to leave the ward with a prostitute he knows from Portland, Candy Starr. As a result of Ratched's denial, McMurphy shatters the replacement glass pane, claiming he did not know it had been replaced. Bromden notes that the nurse shows signs that her patience is starting to wear down. When the glass is replaced again, Scanlon accidentally smashes it with a basketball, which she then throws away.

Doctor Spivey grants McMurphy's request for a pass to take a fishing trip with nine other patients, accompanied by two of his aunts. Men begin to sign up for the trip, each paying McMurphy ten dollars for the boat rental. Meanwhile, Ratched pins newspaper clippings about rough weather and wrecked boats on the bulletin board. Bromden wants to sign the list, but he is afraid to blow his deaf-and-dumb cover, realizing that he has to "keep acting deaf if [he] wanted to hear at all." He remembers that when he was ten, three people came to his home to talk to his father about buying the tribe's land. When Bromden spoke to them, they acted like he had not said a word. This memory represents the first time in a long time that he has remembered something about his childhood.

Geever, an aide, wakes Bromden and McMurphy in the middle of the night when he scrapes off the wads of gum under Bromden's bed. He tells McMurphy that he has tried for a long time to find out where Bromden, as an indigent patient, could obtain gum. After he leaves the dorm, McMurphy gives Bromden some Juicy Fruit, and Bromden, before he can think of what he is doing, thanks him. McMurphy tells him that when he was a boy, he took a job picking beans. The adults ignored him, so McMurphy silently listened to their malicious gossip all summer. At the end of the season, he told everyone what the others said in their absence, creating havoc. Bromden replies that he is too little to do something bold like that.

McMurphy offers to make Bromden big again with his special body-building course. He offers to pay Bromden's share of the fishing trip fee if he promises to get strong enough to lift the control panel in the tub room. He tells Bromden that the aunts who will accompany them are in reality two prostitutes. When McMurphy notices Bromden's erection, he states that Bromden is getting bigger already. Right then, McMurphy adds Bromden's name to the list. The next day he persuades George Sorenson, a former fisherman, to take the last slot.

When Candy arrives at the hospital—without Sandy—the men are transfixed by her beauty and femininity. Ratched threatens to cancel the trip because all the patients cannot fit into Candy's car, and they do not have a second driver. In doing so, she discovers that McMurphy lied about the cost of the rental to make a profit off the other patients. She tries to use this information as part of her typical divide-and-conquer strategy, but the other patients do not seem to mind. McMurphy then persuades Doctor Spivey to come with them and drive the second car. When they stop for gas, the attendant tries to take advantage of them. McMurphy gets out of the car and warns him that they are a bunch of crazy, psychopathic murderers. The other patients, seeing that their illness could actually be a source of power for them, lose their nervousness and follow his lead in using their insanity to intimidate the attendant.

Bromden marvels at the changes the Combine has wrought on the Outside—the thousands of mechanized commuters and houses and children. When they get to the docks, the captain of the boat does not allow them to take the trip, because he does not have a signed waiver exonerating him should any accidents occur. Meanwhile, the men on the dock harass Candy, and the patients are ashamed that they are too afraid to stand up for her. To distract the captain of the boat, McMurphy gives him a phone number to call. When the captain goes to call, McMurphy herds the patients onto the boat. They are already out to sea by the time the captain realizes the number belongs to a brothel.

While on the boat, everyone catches large fish and gets drunk. When they return to the dock, the captain is waiting with some policemen. The doctor threatens to inform the authorities that the captain did not provide enough life jackets, so the policemen leave without arresting anyone. After a short fistfight, McMurphy and the captain have a drink together. The men on the dock are friendly with the patients when they see their impressive catches and after they learn that George is a retired fisherman. Billy is infatuated with Candy; when McMurphy notices this, he arranges a date for them at two in the morning two weeks later, on a Saturday night.

Everyone is in high spirits when they return to the ward, but McMurphy seems pale and exhausted. They had taken a detour to pass by an old, run-down house where McMurphy lived as a child. Caught in a tree branch was an old rag, a remnant from the first time he had sex, as a ten-year-old with a girl who was perhaps even younger than he. She gave him her dress to keep as a reminder, and he threw it out the window, where it caught in a tree branch and remained to this day. Bromden remembers seeing his face reflected in the windshield afterward and remarks how it looked "dreadfully tired and strained and *frantic,* like there was not enough time left for something he had to do."

ANALYSIS

McMurphy's rebellion grows more overt as the patients begin to defy Ratched on their own terms. McMurphy still maintains a somewhat humorous edge to his resistance, as his request for an Accompanied Pass demonstrates. By asking to be let out for a day to consort with a prostitute, McMurphy both asserts his sexuality and reminds Ratched that she has failed to emotionally castrate him. By gaining Spivey's approval for the fishing trip, McMurphy demonstrates to Ratched that he does not deem her the highest authority on the ward. Nurse Ratched can only resist his growing influence by trying in vain to frighten the other patients with the newspaper clippings, which fail to suppress them and their newfound individual thinking.

Meanwhile, Bromden begins to attain greater self-knowledge through McMurphy's influence. He remembers the racist government agents coming to his house, and he realizes the origin of his sense of inadequacy and invisibility. Bromden feels himself becoming stronger as he talks to McMurphy and slowly becomes a man in his own eyes. McMurphy's offer of Juicy Fruit to Bromden illustrates the value of good relationships between the patients, and Bromden's decision to speak demonstrates the extent to which goodwill has helped to heal his wounds.

In contrast, Geever's discovery of Bromden's gum is a reminder that the hospital continues to function like a totalitarian state. The patients are still subject to strict supervision and the invasion of their privacy. Once faced with the conniving Geever, Bromden knows that McMurphy will keep his most precious secret: that he is not deaf and dumb. McMurphy's own childhood experience of playing mute shows that the two of them are more similar than they might appear.

McMurphy's own program of therapy for the other patients involves reviving their faith in their sexuality. He notes, jokingly, that Bromden's erection is proof that he is getting bigger already. McMurphy presents the patients with a woman who can reawaken their repressed sex drives; the pretty Candy Starr, unlike Nurse Ratched, exudes sexuality. McMurphy seems to recognize that the patients, Billy in particular, can become individual, powerful men only if they can experience sexual feelings without the sense of shame that Ratched and the rest of the ward seem to inculcate.

During the trip, two unpleasant experiences threaten the therapeutic value of the outing but ultimately lead to the greatest individual development for the patients. First, when the gas station attendant disrespects them, McMurphy rescues them by showing how their stigmatized identity as mental patients can be used to their advantage. Instead of being made to feel afraid, they can now intimidate others by exaggerating their insanity. McMurphy, in effect, teaches them how to cope with the outside world in a different way, to reject the previously unsuccessful approach of conformity. However, the patients still depend heavily on McMurphy to lead them. When they arrive at the docks, they are too timid to answer the insults of the seamen by themselves.

The second experience that initially seems detrimental, but is actually beneficial, occurs when McMurphy tests the patients by refusing to help them once they are out to sea. Like Christ taking his twelve disciples to the sea, he forces them to fend for themselves, and they find, to their surprise, that they do not actually need his help. They begin to see themselves as men, not as feeble mental patients. When they return to the docks, they realize that they not only have proven something to themselves, but they have proven something to the seamen with their impressive catches. In turn, the seamen act politely and respectfully, in remarkable contrast to their earlier rudeness.

Yet, while the mental state of each patient is improving immensely, the strain of responsibility for curing the patients of their society-generated insecurities has clearly begun to wear McMurphy down. McMurphy's exhaustion seems to stem from something other than the trip alone, and Bromden's description of his expression in the car foreshadows McMurphy's eventual submission. Significantly, this expression occurs in conjunction with McMurphy's childhood memory of being sexually dominated by a woman. Despite all of the fervor and individuality that McMurphy conveys, he also has experienced a distortion of his male sexuality due to a woman's dominance. In his increasing strain, we see that the strength which makes McMurphy so well equipped to combat the mechanistic society of Nurse Ratched—his humanity—is also a weakness that may ultimately lead to his total exhaustion.

PART IV

SUMMARY

Nurse Ratched posts the patients' financial statements on the bulletin board to show that everyone's account, except McMurphy's, shows a steady decline in funds. The other patients begin to question the motivations for his actions. When a phone call keeps McMurphy away from a Group Meeting, Ratched insinuates that everything he does is motivated by the desire for personal gain. Later, Harding argues that they have all gotten their money's worth and that McMurphy never hid his con-man ways from them.

McMurphy asks Bromden if he can move the control panel, as a way of testing how big Bromden has grown. Bromden is able to move it half a foot. McMurphy makes a rigged bet with the other patients that someone could lift the control panel, knowing, of course, that Bromden has already lifted it. Bromden lifts it, and McMurphy wins the bet. Bromden, uncomfortable with McMurphy's deceit, refuses to accept the five dollars that McMurphy offers him later. McMurphy asks why all of a sudden everyone acts like he is a traitor, and Bromden tells him it is because he is always winning things.

Ratched orders that everyone who went on the fishing trip be cleansed because of the company they kept. George has a phobia regarding cleanliness and begs the aides not to spray him with their smelly salve. McMurphy and Bromden get into a fistfight with the aides to defend George, so Ratched sends them to Disturbed. The kind Japanese nurse who tends them explains that army nurses have a habit of trying to run the place as if it were an army hospital and are "a little sick themselves." One of the patients wakes Bromden during the night by yelling in his face, "I'm starting to spin, Indian! Look me, look me!" Bromden wonders how McMurphy can sleep, plagued as he must be by "a hundred faces like that," desperate for his attention.

Nurse Ratched tells McMurphy that he can avoid electroshock therapy by admitting he was wrong. He refuses, telling her "those Chinese Commies could have learned a few things from you, lady." He and Bromden are sent for the treatment, but McMurphy does not seem afraid at all. He voluntarily climbs onto the cross-shaped table and wonders aloud if he will get a "crown of thorns." Bromden, however, is afraid and struggles mightily. During the treatment and afterward, Bromden experiences a rush of images and memories from his childhood. When he regains consciousness, he resists the fog and works to clear his head, the first time he has managed to do so after receiving shock therapy. He knows that this time he "had them beat," and he is not subjected to any more treatments. McMurphy, however, receives three more treatments that week. He maintains an unconcerned attitude about it, but Bromden can tell that the treatments are affecting him. Ratched realizes that McMurphy is growing bigger in the eyes of the other men because he is out of sight, so she decides to bring him back from Disturbed.

The other patients know that Ratched will continue to harass McMurphy, so they urge him to escape. McMurphy reminds them that Billy's date with Candy is later that night. That night, McMurphy persuades Turkle to open the window for Candy. She arrives with Sandy in tow, carrying copious amounts of alcohol. Everyone mixes vodka with cough syrup, while Turkle and McMurphy smoke joints. Sefelt has a seizure while with Sandy, and Harding sprinkles pills over them both, declaring that they are "witnessing the end, the absolute, irrevocable, fantastic end." Sometime after four in the morning, Billy and Candy retreat to the Seclusion Room.

As it gets closer to morning, they realize that they are going to have to figure something out before the staff arrives. Harding tells McMurphy that they can tie up Turkle, so it looks like the mess created by their party was all part of McMurphy's escape attempt. Turkle can keep his job, the other patients will not get into trouble, and McMurphy can drive off to Canada or Mexico with Candy and Sandy. McMurphy asks whether any of the rest of them would want to escape with him. Harding replies by saying that he is almost ready to leave on his own, with all "the traditional red tape." He says that the rest of them are "still sick men in lots of ways. But at least there's that: they are sick *men* now. No more rabbits, Mack."

McMurphy and Sandy climb into bed after asking Turkle to wake them up right before the morning staff arrives. Unfortunately, Turkle falls asleep, and the aides discover them in the morning. Bromden surmises that the ensuing repercussions were inevitable, whether or not they followed through with McMurphy's escape. He figures that even if McMurphy had escaped, he would have had to come back and not let the nurse get "the last play."

The next morning all the patients are incredulous about the night's activities. As Ratched turns up more and more incriminating remnants from the party, the patients cannot keep their laughter in, and the nurse looks like she is going to "blow up like a bladder." McMurphy has a chance to escape when Turkle undoes the screen to let Sandy out, but he refuses, despite Harding's warnings of what is to come. When Ratched finds Billy with Candy, he is calm and peaceful. He and Candy both move "like cats full of warm milk." The nurse threatens to tell Billy's mother. Billy regains his stutter and begins to cry, begging her to keep it a secret and blaming Candy, McMurphy, and Harding for the whole thing. She sends him to Spivey's office to wait while she clears things up with the other patients. But Billy ends up committing suicide by cutting his throat.

Nurse Ratched asks McMurphy if he is satisfied with his accomplishments, and then she retreats to the Nurses' Station. Bromden realizes that nobody will be able to stop McMurphy from rebelling, because it is the need of the patients that has been encouraging him all along, "making him wink and grin and laugh and go on with his act long after his humor had been parched dry between two electrodes." Then, McMurphy smashes through the glass door, rips open the front of Ratched's uniform, and tries to strangle her. As he is pried off of the nurse, he gives out a cry "of cornered-animal fear and hate and surrender and defiance."

Several of the Acutes transfer to other wards, and some check themselves out of the hospital altogether. The doctor is asked to resign but refuses. Ratched returns after a week on medical leave with a heavy bandage around her throat, unable to speak. She cannot regain her former power over the ward. Eventually the only patients left on the ward are Bromden, Martini, and Scanlon. McMurphy is given a lobotomy for his attack on Nurse Ratched. When he is returned to the ward after the operation, he is a vegetable. That same night, Bromden suffocates McMurphy with a pillow. He throws

the control panel through a window screen and escapes from the hospital, hitching a ride with a trucker.

ANALYSIS

Ratched makes one last feeble attempt to regain control when she uses the same principle she used earlier to ensure the patients' submission to her authority: divide and conquer. She begins to sow the seeds of distrust among the patients by publicizing the financial gain McMurphy has enjoyed since his transfer from the work farm. Harding defends McMurphy, pointing out that McMurphy has more than repaid the patients' financial losses by providing them with the means to resist Ratched's influence.

But it is McMurphy's timing of the rigged bet on the control panel that proves extremely disadvantageous. He fleeces them of their money too soon after Ratched has planted the seeds of doubt in their minds. Bromden is affected most acutely, because he feels that McMurphy has used him to take advantage of the others. Only after McMurphy regains the patients' trust by taking on yet another personal risk for their benefit—defending George against the aides—do Bromden and the others realize McMurphy's true objectives. Even Bromden helps this time, demonstrating the extent to which he has regained his self-confidence.

McMurphy's self-sacrifice for the benefit of the other patients begins to surface after he defends George, and also when he undergoes the electroshock treatments. McMurphy is belted to a cross-shaped table, an obvious allusion to a crucifix. This Christ imagery suggests an impending martyrdom on the part of McMurphy, and he even compares himself to Christ when he asks whether he gets to wear a crown of thorns. Of course, a martyr ultimately must sacrifice himself to save others. This proves true, since although Bromden feels strong enough to withstand the effects of the electroshock, McMurphy weakens under the repeated treatments. Bromden finally begins to feel that his victory over the hospital is complete. He is no longer ruled by his fears or his past, thanks to the help of his unlikely savior, McMurphy.

After Nurse Ratched provokes Billy, leading to his suicide, McMurphy truly does become a Christ figure for the patients. Under the invisible but heavy pressure of the other patients' expectations, McMurphy makes the ultimate sacrifice to ensure that Ratched cannot use Billy's death to undo everything they have gained. By attacking Ratched and ripping her uniform, he permanently breaks her power but also forfeits his own life. Though Ratched tries to give McMurphy a fate worse than death by having him lobotomized, Bromden dignifies McMurphy by killing him, assuring that McMurphy will always be a symbol of resistance instead of a lingering cautionary tale for future patients on Ratched's ward.

Important Quotations Explained

1. I been silent so long now it's gonna roar out of me like floodwaters and you think the guy telling this is ranting and raving my God; you think this is too horrible to have really happened, this is too awful to be the truth! But, please. It's still hard for me to have a clear mind thinking on it. But it's the truth even if it didn't happen.

We are given this brainteaser from Chief Bromden in Part 1. The reader has already gotten a glimpse of Bromden's paranoia, from the novel's opening lines, as well as a sense that he is not seeing things from an everyday perspective. For example, Bromden describes Nurse Ratched transforming into a huge machine, and he has to be sedated when the aides try to shave him and he starts screaming "Air Raid." Up until this point he has not addressed the reader directly; it is as though we are overhearing his private thoughts. But in this passage he asserts himself as not only the narrator but the author of the story. We learn here that he has an important story to tell, even though it is going to be difficult. The ugly and violent images that he has already shown us, he warns us, are just a taste of what is to come.

The last line of the quote is Bromden's request that the reader keep an open mind. His hallucinations provide metaphorical insight into the hidden realities of the hospital and should not be overlooked simply because they did not actually happen. Although over the course of the novel Bromden regains his sanity, he still witnesses many of the events while in a semi-catatonic, hallucinatory state; we have to trust in the truth of his sharp perceptions, no matter what form they take.

2.   The flock gets sight of a spot of blood on some chicken
     and they all go to peckin' at it, see, till they rip the chicken
     to shreds, blood and bones and feathers. But usually a
     couple of the flock gets spotted in the fracas, then it's their
     turn. And a few more gets spots and gets pecked to death,
     and more and more. Oh, a peckin' party can wipe out the
     whole flock in a matter of a few hours, buddy, I seen it. A
     mighty awesome sight. The only way to prevent it—with
     chickens—is to clip blinders on them. So's they can't see.

McMurphy gives this explanation to Harding and the other patients
in Part 1 after his first Group Meeting. The entire group had been
tearing into Harding, adhering to Doctor Spivey's theory of the
"Therapeutic Community," where the patients are encouraged to
bring "old sins out into the open." Afterward, McMurphy tells the
other patients that they were like "a bunch of chickens at a peckin'
party," attacking the weakest one with such blind fury that they all
put themselves in danger.

   McMurphy is immediately shocked by the behavior of the patients and staff. It is clear to him that Ratched maintains her power
through such strategies as divide and conquer. He points out that
she "pecks the first peck," or points out the first weakness, and then
just sits back and watches as the patients start to attack each other.
He does not understand why the patients fall for this strategy, especially since they might be next in line as the object of ridicule. The
patients do seem to have blinders on; they are so blinded by their
own shame that they are unable to see Ratched's true nature and the
way she manipulates and controls them so effortlessly.

3. So you see my friend, it is somewhat as you stated: man
    has but one truly effective weapon against the juggernaut
    of modern matriarchy, but it certainly is not laughter.
    One weapon, and with every passing year in this hip,
    motivationally researched society, more and more people
    are discovering how to render that weapon useless and
    conquer those who have hitherto been conquerors. . . .

This passage occurs later in the same discussion that followed
McMurphy's first Group Meeting in Part 1. Here, Kesey begins to
develop his misogynistic theory about modern society. Harding is
talking to McMurphy, explaining that men's one weapon against
women is the penis, and that if men are unable to use rape effectively, they have no chance to regain power in society. Kesey believes
that women have learned this, and they now know how to render
men's one weapon useless—in other words, they are all ball-cutters.
Where rape is the male means to power, castration is the female way
to domination.

These crude ideas are given substance throughout the novel. Kesey uses McMurphy's fearless sexuality as a sign that he is sane.
McMurphy goads Ratched sexually by wearing just a towel, pinch-
ing her rear, remarking on her breasts, and eventually tearing her
shirt open. Most of the male patients have stories about damaging
relationships with women, such as Bromden's mother, Billy Bibbit's
mother and onetime girlfriend, and Harding's wife. When McMurphy notices Bromden's erection, a sign that he is "getting bigger
already," it signifies that Bromden is becoming more powerful and
saner. Similarly, through sex with Candy, Billy briefly regains his
confidence and his manhood, until Ratched takes it away and he
commits suicide. Moreover, Ratched and the hospital supervisor,
also a woman, wield all the power in the hospital: "We are victims
of a matriarchy here," says Harding.

4. Except the sun, on these three strangers, is all of a sudden
    way the hell brighter than usual and I can see the . . . seams
    where they're put together. And, almost, see the apparatus
    inside them take the words I just said and try to fit the
    words in here and there, this place and that, and when they
    find the words don't have any place ready-made where
    they'll fit, the machinery disposes of the words like they
    weren't even spoken.

In this passage from the beginning of Part III, Bromden, who has
been gaining self-awareness since McMurphy's arrival on the ward,
remembers a scarring experience he had as a ten-year-old. Three
government officials came to speak to his father, Chief Tee Ah Millatoona, about buying the tribe's land to build a hydroelectric dam.
When Bromden tried to speak to them, he noticed that "[n]ot a one
of the three acts like they heard a thing [he] said." He begins to see
the world differently, believing that he can see the seams on people,
as though they were inhuman or machine-like.

For Kesey, the drones who do the dirty work of an oppressive
society are basically machines. The government officials who vis-
ited Bromden's father were planning to make a profit by destroying
nature, represented by the tribe's ancient connection to the land,
the river, and the fish, and replacing it with destructive technology.
The brightness of the sun sheds light on the dark fact these officials
taught Bromden: that people who do not have "any place ready-
made where they'll fit" are ignored and disposed of. At first the
"machinery" disposes of Bromden's words; then, over time, it seems
to ignore his entire being.

QUOTATIONS

5.   While McMurphy laughs. Rocking farther and farther
     backward against the cabin top, spreading his laugh out
     across the water—laughing at the girl, the guys, at George,
     at me sucking my bleeding thumb, at the captain back at
     the pier and the bicycle rider and the service-station guys
     and the five thousand houses and the Big Nurse and all of
     it. Because he knows you have to laugh at the things that
     hurt you just to keep yourself in balance, just to keep the
     world from running you plumb crazy.

While on the fishing expedition, the patients are able to laugh freely
and feel like whole humans again. As usual, this happens with Mc-
Murphy's guidance—he is an example for all the patients to follow.
Here, Bromden shows how McMurphy's booming laughter in the
face of chaos, which could be seen as the mark of a psychopath, is
the one thing that keeps McMurphy sane.

   Bromden implies that it is the pressures of society—the captain, the five thousand houses, the Big Nurse, "the things that hurt
you"—that drive people insane. To maintain sanity in such an oppressive and cruel world, people cannot allow these external forces
to exert too much power. When a person succumbs to seeing and
experiencing all the sadness and suffering of humanity, as Bromden
has done for ten years, it naturally makes him or her unable, or
unwilling, to cope with reality—in other words, it can make that
person "plumb crazy."

QUOTATIONS

KEY FACTS

FULL TITLE
One Flew Over the Cuckoo's Nest

AUTHOR
Ken Kesey

TYPE OF WORK
Novel

GENRE
Allegorical novel; counterculture novel; protest novel

LANGUAGE
English

TIME AND PLACE WRITTEN
The late 1950s; at Stanford University in California while Kesey was enrolled in the creative writing program, working as an orderly in a psychiatric ward, and participating in experimental LSD trials

DATE OF FIRST PUBLICATION
1962

PUBLISHER
Viking Press

NARRATOR
Chief Bromden, also known as Chief Broom, who tells the story after he has escaped from the hospital

POINT OF VIEW
Chief Bromden narrates in the first person. He tells the story as it appears to him, though his objectivity is somewhat compromised by the fact that he suffers from paranoia and hallucinations. His unusual state of mind provides metaphorical insight into the insidious reality of the hospital as well as society in general. Because he pretends to be deaf and dumb, he is privy to secret staff information that is kept from other patients, which makes him a more reliable narrator than any other patient would be.

TONE

The novel's tone is critical and allegorical; the hospital is presented as a metaphor for the oppressive society of the late 1950s. The novel praises the expression of sexuality as the ultimate goal and denounces repression as based on fear and hate. Bromden's psychedelic and slightly paranoid worldview may be commensurate with Kesey's, and McMurphy's use of mischief and humor to undermine authority also seems to echo the author's attitudes.

TENSE

Present

SETTING (TIME)

1950s

SETTING (PLACE)

A mental hospital in Oregon

PROTAGONIST

Randle P. McMurphy

MAJOR CONFLICT

The patients in the mental ward are cowed and repressed by the emasculating Nurse Ratched, who represents the oppressive force of modern society. McMurphy tries to lead them to rebel against her authority by asserting their individuality and sexuality, while Nurse Ratched attempts to discredit McMurphy and shame the patients back into docility.

RISING ACTION

The World Series rebellion; McMurphy's encounter with the lifeguard; McMurphy discovering what being committed means; Cheswick's death

CLIMAX

McMurphy reasserts himself against Nurse Ratched at the end of Part II by smashing the glass window in the Nurses' Station, signaling that his rebellion is no longer lighthearted or selfish but committed and violent. McMurphy takes on the responsibility for rehabilitating the other patients.

FALLING ACTION

McMurphy's decision to return Bromden to his former strength; the fishing trip and visit to McMurphy's childhood

KEY FACTS

house, where Bromden sees his panic and fatigue; McMurphy
and Bromden's fight with the aides; the electroshock therapy;
the ward party and Billy's suicide; McMurphy's violent attack
on Nurse Ratched; the lobotomy

THEMES
Women as castrators; society's destruction of natural impulses;
the importance of expressing sexuality; false diagnoses of
insanity

MOTIFS
Invisibility; the power of laughter; real versus imagined size

SYMBOLS
The fog machine; McMurphy's boxer shorts; the electroshock
therapy table

FORESHADOWING
The story of Maxwell Taber; the electroshock therapy table
shaped like a cross; the deaths of Rawler, Cheswick, and Billy;
Bromden's dreams and hallucinations

Study Questions

1. *How does Kesey make the reader question the accepted definitions of "sane," "insane," "sick," and "healthy"?*

Bromden sees modern society as an oppressive, mechanizing force, and he views the hospital as a repair shop for the people who do not fit into their roles as cogs in the machine. His way of interpreting the world emphasizes the social pressure to conform. Those who do not conform to the rules and conventions of society are considered defective products of the "schools, churches, and neighborhoods." Such people are labeled mentally ill and sent for treatment. The hospital is normally defined as the place where the ill go to be cured. However, in the cases of Ellis, Ruckly, and Taber, the cure—being in the psychiatric hospital—is obviously worse than the disease. Ellis and Ruckly are considered "failures," but Taber is considered a success. However, it is hard to tell the difference between the cured and sick patients. Taber, the cured patient, functions like a robot incapable of independent thought after he leaves the hospital; as such, he fits perfectly into society.

2. *Why is the fishing trip therapeutic for the patients?*

When the gas station attendant tries to intimidate the patients and the doctor into accepting services they do not want, McMurphy comes to their rescue by showing them how their stigmatized identity as mental patients can be used to their advantage. Instead of being made to feel afraid, they can inspire fear in others by exaggerating their insanity. McMurphy tries to teach the other patients another way to cope with the outside world, without using an approach of total conformity. However, when they arrive at the docks, they are too timid to answer the insults of the seamen without the support of McMurphy. Once they are out to sea, McMurphy refuses to step in and aid the patients. He leaves them to manage things for themselves, and, to their surprise, they find they do not actually need his help. They begin to see themselves as men, not as feeble mental patients. When the patients return to the docks, they realize that they have proven something to themselves and to the outside world, and the seamen are impressed by their large catches from the sea.

3. How does McMurphy become a Christ figure?

Several images contribute to the perception of McMurphy as a Christ figure. He is baptized with a shower upon entering the ward. He takes the patients on a fishing trip, like Jesus and his twelve disciples, to test and strengthen their faith in him and his rehabilitation methods. When McMurphy is taken to get electroshock treatment, he lies down voluntarily on the cross-shaped table and asks whether he will get his "crown of thorns." Under the weighty pressure of the other patients' expectations, McMurphy makes the ultimate sacrifice to ensure that Ratched cannot use Billy's death to undo everything they have gained. He sacrifices his own hopes of personal salvation when he violently attacks her. McMurphy rips her uniform to reveal her femininity, the evidence that she is not an all-powerful machine but a flesh-and-blood person. His deed succeeds in destroying Ratched's power. Although he himself dies as a result, his sacrifice becomes an inspiration to the other patients.

How to Write
Literary Analysis

The Literary Essay: A Step-by-Step Guide

When you read for pleasure, your only goal is enjoyment. You might find yourself reading to get caught up in an exciting story, to learn about an interesting time or place, or just to pass time. Maybe you're looking for inspiration, guidance, or a reflection of your own life. There are as many different, valid ways of reading a book as there are books in the world.

When you read a work of literature in an English class, however, you're being asked to read in a special way: you're being asked to perform *literary analysis*. To analyze something means to break it down into smaller parts and then examine how those parts work, both individually and together. Literary analysis involves examining all the parts of a novel, play, short story, or poem—elements such as character, setting, tone, and imagery—and thinking about how the author uses those elements to create certain effects.

A literary essay isn't a book review: you're not being asked whether or not you liked a book or whether you'd recommend it to another reader. A literary essay also isn't like the kind of book report you wrote when you were younger, where your teacher wanted you to summarize the book's action. A high school- or college-level literary essay asks, "How does this piece of literature actually work?" "How does it do what it does?" and, "Why might the author have made the choices he or she did?"

The Seven Steps
No one is born knowing how to analyze literature; it's a skill you learn and a process you can master. As you gain more practice with this kind of thinking and writing, you'll be able to craft a method that works best for you. But until then, here are seven basic steps to writing a well-constructed literary essay:

1. Ask questions
2. Collect evidence
3. Construct a thesis

4. Develop and organize arguments
5. Write the introduction
6. Write the body paragraphs
7. Write the conclusion

---

1. ASK QUESTIONS

When you're assigned a literary essay in class, your teacher will often provide you with a list of writing prompts. Lucky you! Now all you have to do is choose one. Do yourself a favor and pick a topic that interests you. You'll have a much better (not to mention easier) time if you start off with something you enjoy thinking about. If you are asked to come up with a topic by yourself, though, you might start to feel a little panicked. Maybe you have too many ideas—or none at all. Don't worry. Take a deep breath and start by asking yourself these questions:

- **What struck you?** Did a particular image, line, or scene linger in your mind for a long time? If it fascinated you, chances are you can draw on it to write a fascinating essay.

- **What confused you?** Maybe you were surprised to see a character act in a certain way, or maybe you didn't understand why the book ended the way it did. Confusing moments in a work of literature are like a loose thread in a sweater: if you pull on it, you can unravel the entire thing. Ask yourself why the author chose to write about that character or scene the way he or she did and you might tap into some important insights about the work as a whole.

- **Did you notice any patterns?** Is there a phrase that the main character uses constantly or an image that repeats throughout the book? If you can figure out how that pattern weaves through the work and what the significance of that pattern is, you've almost got your entire essay mapped out.

- **Did you notice any contradictions or ironies?** Great works of literature are complex; great literary essays recognize and explain those complexities. Maybe the title (*Happy Days*) totally disagrees with the book's subject matter (hungry orphans dying in the woods). Maybe the main character acts one way around his family and a completely different way around his friends and associates. If you can find a way to explain a work's contradictory elements, you've got the seeds of a great essay.

At this point, you don't need to know exactly what you're going to say about your topic; you just need a place to begin your exploration. You can help direct your reading and brainstorming by formulating your topic as a *question*, which you'll then try to answer in your essay. The best questions invite critical debates and discussions, not just a rehashing of the summary. Remember, you're looking for something you can *prove or argue* based on evidence you find in the text. Finally, remember to keep the scope of your question in mind: is this a topic you can adequately address within the word or page limit you've been given? Conversely, is this a topic big enough to fill the required length?

GOOD QUESTIONS

> *"Are Romeo and Juliet's parents responsible for the deaths of their children?"*
> *"Why do pigs keep showing up in* LORD OF THE FLIES?"
> *"Are Dr. Frankenstein and his monster alike? How?"*

BAD QUESTIONS

> *"What happens to Scout in* TO KILL A MOCKINGBIRD?"
> *"What do the other characters in* JULIUS CAESAR *think about Caesar?"*
> *"How does Hester Prynne in* THE SCARLET LETTER *remind me of my sister?"*

---

2. COLLECT EVIDENCE

Once you know what question you want to answer, it's time to scour the book for things that will help you answer the question. Don't worry if you don't know what you want to say yet—right now you're just collecting ideas and material and letting it all percolate. Keep track of passages, symbols, images, or scenes that deal with your topic. Eventually, you'll start making connections between these examples and your thesis will emerge.

Here's a brief summary of the various parts that compose each and every work of literature. These are the elements that you will analyze in your essay, and which you will offer as evidence to support your arguments. For more on the parts of literary works, see the Glossary of Literary Terms at the end of this section.

ELEMENTS OF STORY These are the *what*s of the work—what happens, where it happens, and to whom it happens.

- **Plot:** All of the events and actions of the work.

- **Character:** The people who act and are acted upon in a literary work. The main character of a work is known as the *protagonist*.

- **Conflict:** The central tension in the work. In most cases, the protagonist wants something, while opposing forces (antagonists) hinder the protagonist's progress.

- **Setting:** When and where the work takes place. Elements of setting include location, time period, time of day, weather, social atmosphere, and economic conditions.

- **Narrator:** The person telling the story. The narrator may straightforwardly report what happens, convey the subjective opinions and perceptions of one or more characters, or provide commentary and opinion in his or her own voice.

- **Themes:** The main idea or message of the work—usually an abstract idea about people, society, or life in general. A work may have many themes, which may be in tension with one another.

ELEMENTS OF STYLE These are the *how*s—how the characters speak, how the story is constructed, and how language is used throughout the work.

- **Structure and organization:** How the parts of the work are assembled. Some novels are narrated in a linear, chronological fashion, while others skip around in time. Some plays follow a traditional three- or five-act structure, while others are a series of loosely connected scenes. Some authors deliberately leave gaps in their works, leaving readers to puzzle out the missing information. A work's structure and organization can tell you a lot about the kind of message it wants to convey.

- **Point of view:** The perspective from which a story is told. In *first-person point of view,* the narrator involves him or herself in the story. ("I went to the store"; "We watched in horror as the bird slammed into the window.") A first-person narrator is usually the protagonist of the work, but not always. In *third-person point of view,* the narrator does not participate

in the story. A third-person narrator may closely follow a specific character, recounting that individual character's thoughts or experiences, or it may be what we call an *omniscient* narrator. Omniscient narrators see and know all: they can witness any event in any time or place and are privy to the inner thoughts and feelings of all characters. Remember that the narrator and the author are not the same thing!

- **Diction:** Word choice. Whether a character uses dry, clinical language or flowery prose with lots of exclamation points can tell you a lot about his or her attitude and personality.

- **Syntax:** Word order and sentence construction. Syntax is a crucial part of establishing an author's narrative voice. Ernest Hemingway, for example, is known for writing in very short, straightforward sentences, while James Joyce characteristically wrote in long, incredibly complicated lines.

- **Tone:** The mood or feeling of the text. Diction and syntax often contribute to the tone of a work. A novel written in short, clipped sentences that use small, simple words might feel brusque, cold, or matter-of-fact.

- **Imagery:** Language that appeals to the senses, representing things that can be seen, smelled, heard, tasted, or touched.

- **Figurative language:** Language that is not meant to be interpreted literally. The most common types of figurative language are *metaphors* and *similes,* which compare two unlike things in order to suggest a similarity between them—for example, "All the world's a stage," or "The moon is like a ball of green cheese." (Metaphors say one thing *is* another thing; similes claim that one thing is *like* another thing.)

---

3. Construct a Thesis

When you've examined all the evidence you've collected and know how you want to answer the question, it's time to write your thesis statement. A *thesis* is a claim about a work of literature that needs to be supported by evidence and arguments. The thesis statement is the heart of the literary essay, and the bulk of your paper will be spent trying to prove this claim. A good thesis will be:

- **Arguable.** "*The Great Gatsby* describes New York society in the 1920s" isn't a thesis—it's a fact.

- **Provable through textual evidence.** "*Hamlet* is a confusing but ultimately very well-written play" is a weak thesis because it offers the writer's personal opinion about the book. Yes, it's arguable, but it's not a claim that can be proved or supported with examples taken from the play itself.

- **Surprising.** "Both George and Lenny change a great deal in *Of Mice and Men*" is a weak thesis because it's obvious. A really strong thesis will argue for a reading of the text that is not immediately apparent.

- **Specific.** "Dr. Frankenstein's monster tells us a lot about the human condition" is *almost* a really great thesis statement, but it's still too vague. What does the writer mean by "a lot"? *How* does the monster tell us so much about the human condition?

GOOD THESIS STATEMENTS

Question: In *Romeo and Juliet*, which is more powerful in shaping the lovers' story: fate or foolishness?

Thesis: "Though Shakespeare defines Romeo and Juliet as 'star-crossed lovers' and images of stars and planets appear throughout the play, a closer examination of that celestial imagery reveals that the stars are merely witnesses to the characters' foolish activities and not the causes themselves."

Question: How does the bell jar function as a symbol in Sylvia Plath's *The Bell Jar*?

Thesis: "A bell jar is a bell-shaped glass that has three basic uses: to hold a specimen for observation, to contain gases, and to maintain a vacuum. The bell jar appears in each of these capacities in *The Bell Jar*, Plath's semi-autobiographical novel, and each appearance marks a different stage in Esther's mental breakdown."

Question: Would Piggy in *The Lord of the Flies* make a good island leader if he were given the chance?

Thesis: "Though the intelligent, rational, and innovative Piggy has the mental characteristics of a good leader, he ultimately lacks the social skills necessary to be an effective one. Golding emphasizes this point by giving Piggy a foil in the charismatic Jack, whose magnetic personality allows him to capture and wield power effectively, if not always wisely."

4. DEVELOP AND ORGANIZE ARGUMENTS

The reasons and examples that support your thesis will form the middle paragraphs of your essay. Since you can't really write your thesis statement until you know how you'll structure your argument, you'll probably end up working on steps 3 and 4 at the same time.

There's no single method of argumentation that will work in every context. One essay prompt might ask you to compare and contrast two characters, while another asks you to trace an image through a given work of literature. These questions require different kinds of answers and therefore different kinds of arguments. Below, we'll discuss three common kinds of essay prompts and some strategies for constructing a solid, well-argued case.

TYPES OF LITERARY ESSAYS

- **Compare and contrast**

    Compare and contrast the characters of Huck and Jim in THE ADVENTURES OF HUCKLEBERRY FINN.

    Chances are you've written this kind of essay before. In an academic literary context, you'll organize your arguments the same way you would in any other class. You can either go *subject by subject* or *point by point*. In the former, you'll discuss one character first and then the second. In the latter, you'll choose several traits (attitude toward life, social status, images and metaphors associated with the character) and devote a paragraph to each. You may want to use a mix of these two approaches—for example, you may want to spend a paragraph a piece broadly sketching Huck's and Jim's personalities before transitioning into a paragraph or two that describes a few key points of comparison. This can be a highly effective strategy if you want to make a counterintuitive argument—that, despite seeming to be totally different, the two objects being compared are actually similar in a very important way (or vice versa). Remember that your essay should reveal something fresh or unexpected about the text, so think beyond the obvious parallels and differences.

- **Trace**

    Choose an image—for example, birds, knives, or eyes—and trace that image throughout MACBETH.

    Sounds pretty easy, right? All you need to do is read the play, underline every appearance of a knife in *Macbeth,* and then list them in your essay in the order they appear, right? Well, not exactly. Your teacher doesn't want a simple catalog of examples. He or she wants to see you make *connections* between those examples—that's the difference between summarizing and analyzing. In the *Macbeth* example above, think about the different contexts in which knives appear in the play and to what effect. In *Macbeth*, there are real knives and imagined knives; knives that kill and knives that simply threaten. Categorize and classify your examples to give them some order. Finally, always keep the overall effect in mind. After you choose and analyze your examples, you should come to some greater understanding about the work, as well as your chosen image, symbol, or phrase's role in developing the major themes and stylistic strategies of that work.

- **Debate**

  Is the society depicted in 1984 good for its citizens?

  In this kind of essay, you're being asked to debate a moral, ethical, or aesthetic issue regarding the work. You might be asked to judge a character or group of characters (*Is Caesar responsible for his own demise?*) or the work itself (*Is* JANE EYRE *a feminist novel?*). For this kind of essay, there are two important points to keep in mind. First, don't simply base your arguments on your personal feelings and reactions. Every literary essay expects you to read and analyze the work, so search for evidence in the text. What do characters in *1984* have to say about the government of Oceania? What images does Orwell use that might give you a hint about his attitude toward the government? As in any debate, you also need to make sure that you define all the necessary terms before you begin to argue your case. What does it mean to be a "good" society? What makes a novel "feminist"? You should define your terms right up front, in the first paragraph after your introduction.

  Second, remember that strong literary essays make contrary and surprising arguments. Try to think outside the box. In the *1984* example above, it seems like the obvious answer would be no, the totalitarian society depicted in Orwell's novel is *not* good for its citizens. But can you think of any arguments for the opposite side? Even if your final assertion is that the novel depicts a cruel, repressive, and therefore harmful society, acknowledging and responding to the counterargument will strengthen your overall case.

5. WRITE THE INTRODUCTION

Your introduction sets up the entire essay. It's where you present your topic and articulate the particular issues and questions you'll be addressing. It's also where you, as the writer, introduce yourself to your readers. A persuasive literary essay immediately establishes its writer as a knowledgeable, authoritative figure.

An introduction can vary in length depending on the overall length of the essay, but in a traditional five-paragraph essay it should be no longer than one paragraph. However long it is, your introduction needs to:

- **Provide any necessary context.** Your introduction should situate the reader and let him or her know what to expect. What book are you discussing? Which characters? What topic will you be addressing?

- **Answer the "So what?" question.** Why is this topic important, and why is your particular position on the topic noteworthy? Ideally, your introduction should pique the reader's interest by suggesting how your argument is surprising or otherwise counterintuitive. Literary essays make unexpected connections and reveal less-than-obvious truths.

- **Present your thesis.** This usually happens at or very near the end of your introduction.

- **Indicate the shape of the essay to come.** Your reader should finish reading your introduction with a good sense of the scope of your essay as well as the path you'll take toward proving your thesis. You don't need to spell out every step, but you do need to suggest the organizational pattern you'll be using.

Your introduction should not:

- **Be vague.** Beware of the two killer words in literary analysis: *interesting* and *important*. Of course the work, question, or example is interesting and important—that's why you're writing about it!

- **Open with any grandiose assertions.** Many student readers think that beginning their essays with a flamboyant statement such as, "Since the dawn of time, writers have been fascinated with the topic of free will," makes them

sound important and commanding. You know what? It
actually sounds pretty amateurish.

- **Wildly praise the work.** Another typical mistake student
  writers make is extolling the work or author. Your teacher
  doesn't need to be told that "Shakespeare is perhaps the
  greatest writer in the English language." You can mention
  a work's reputation in passing—by referring to *The Adventures of Huckleberry Finn* as "Mark Twain's enduring
  classic," for example—but don't make a point of bringing it
  up unless that reputation is key to your argument.

- **Go off-topic.** Keep your introduction streamlined and to
  the point. Don't feel the need to throw in all kinds of bells
  and whistles in order to impress your reader—just get to the
  point as quickly as you can, without skimping on any of the
  required steps.

6. WRITE THE BODY PARAGRAPHS

Once you've written your introduction, you'll take the arguments
you developed in step 4 and turn them into your body paragraphs.
The organization of this middle section of your essay will largely be
determined by the argumentative strategy you use, but no matter
how you arrange your thoughts, your body paragraphs need to do
the following:

- **Begin with a strong topic sentence.** Topic sentences are like
  signs on a highway: they tell the reader where they are and
  where they're going. A good topic sentence not only alerts
  readers to what issue will be discussed in the following
  paragraph but also gives them a sense of what argument
  will be made *about* that issue. "Rumor and gossip play an
  important role in *The Crucible*" isn't a strong topic sentence
  because it doesn't tell us very much. "The community's
  constant gossiping creates an environment that allows false
  accusations to flourish" is a much stronger topic sentence—
  it not only tells us *what* the paragraph will discuss (gossip)
  but *how* the paragraph will discuss the topic (by showing
  how gossip creates a set of conditions that leads to the play's
  climactic action).

- **Fully and completely develop a single thought.** Don't skip
  around in your paragraph or try to stuff in too much
  material. Body paragraphs are like bricks: each individual

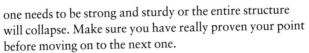

one needs to be strong and sturdy or the entire structure will collapse. Make sure you have really proven your point before moving on to the next one.

- **Use transitions effectively.** Good literary essay writers know that each paragraph must be clearly and strongly linked to the material around it. Think of each paragraph as a response to the one that precedes it. Use transition words and phrases such as *however, similarly, on the contrary, therefore,* and *furthermore* to indicate what kind of response you're making.

---

7. WRITE THE CONCLUSION

Just as you used the introduction to ground your readers in the topic before providing your thesis, you'll use the conclusion to quickly summarize the specifics learned thus far and then hint at the broader implications of your topic. A good conclusion will:

- **Do more than simply restate the thesis.** If your thesis argued that *The Catcher in the Rye* can be read as a Christian allegory, don't simply end your essay by saying, "And that is why *The Catcher in the Rye* can be read as a Christian allegory." If you've constructed your arguments well, this kind of statement will just be redundant.

- **Synthesize the arguments, not summarize them.** Similarly, don't repeat the details of your body paragraphs in your conclusion. The reader has already read your essay, and chances are it's not so long that they've forgotten all your points by now.

- **Revisit the "So what?" question.** In your introduction, you made a case for why your topic and position are important. You should close your essay with the same sort of gesture. What do your readers know now that they didn't know before? How will that knowledge help them better appreciate or understand the work overall?

- **Move from the specific to the general.** Your essay has most likely treated a very specific element of the work—a single character, a small set of images, or a particular passage. In your conclusion, try to show how this narrow discussion has wider implications for the work overall. If your essay on *To Kill a Mockingbird* focused on the character of Boo Radley, for example, you might want to include a bit in your conclusion about how he fits into the novel's larger message about childhood, innocence, or family life.

- **Stay relevant.** Your conclusion should suggest new directions of thought, but it shouldn't be treated as an opportunity to pad your essay with all the extra, interesting ideas you came up with during your brainstorming sessions but couldn't fit into the essay proper. Don't attempt to stuff in unrelated queries or too many abstract thoughts.

- **Avoid making overblown closing statements.** A conclusion should open up your highly specific, focused discussion, but it should do so without drawing a sweeping lesson about life or human nature. Making such observations may be part of the point of reading, but it's almost always a mistake in essays, where these observations tend to sound overly dramatic or simply silly.

A+ Essay Checklist

Congratulations! If you've followed all the steps we've outlined above, you should have a solid literary essay to show for all your efforts. What if you've got your sights set on an A+? To write the kind of superlative essay that will be rewarded with a perfect grade, keep the following rubric in mind. These are the qualities that teachers expect to see in a truly A+ essay. How does yours stack up?

- ✓ Demonstrates a thorough understanding of the book
- ✓ Presents an original, compelling argument
- ✓ Thoughtfully analyzes the text's formal elements
- ✓ Uses appropriate and insightful examples
- ✓ Structures ideas in a logical and progressive order
- ✓ Demonstrates a mastery of sentence construction, transitions, grammar, spelling, and word choice

SUGGESTED ESSAY TOPICS

1. *How is Nurse Ratched's ward like a totalitarian society?*

2. ONE FLEW OVER THE CUCKOO'S NEST *has been criticized for its treatment of race and gender. Why do you think this is the case?*

3. *McMurphy, Colonel Matterson, and Bromden are war veterans. Nurse Ratched is a former army nurse who tries to run her ward as if it were an army hospital. How might the advent of modern warfare serve as a metaphor for the sickness that Kesey perceives in modern society?*

4. *Why is Bromden the narrator of* ONE FLEW OVER THE CUCKOO'S NEST *instead of McMurphy? Who is the real protagonist of the novel? How does the use of Bromden as the narrator tie into the biblical allusions in the novel?*

LITERARY ANALYSIS

A+ Student Essay

> Contrast Nurse Ratched with McMurphy. What values do they represent? How does the pairing of these antagonistic characters illuminate major themes in the novel?

In *One Flew over the Cuckoo's Nest,* Nurse Ratched represents the virtues of self-repression and conformity, of obeying society's rules without question or complaint. By contrast, McMurphy stands for the ideals of individuality and self-expression. He represents the importance of asserting one's thoughts and eccentricities without fear of upsetting a status quo. Several of Kesey's secondary characters, such as Harding, Pete, and Chief Bromden, experience conflicts between their terror of Nurse Ratched and their admiration for McMurphy. The competing philosophies of nurse and disobedient patient thus reinforce Kesey's idea that many people are unsure when to rebel and when to conform, dissatisfied with the world they inhabit yet afraid to state their wishes and advocate change.

Nurse Ratched's statements and actions suggest that individuality is wrong and that the noblest goal is to fit into society's mainstream. Bromden likens Ratched to an engineer, altering the gears of her patients until they are fully robotic, compliant, and able to function in the world without causing a scene. Nobody dares laugh on Ratched's watch, because such an assertion of personality would lead to questioning and a harsh reprimand from the Big Nurse. Ratched has hung a "plaque of cooperation" in her ward, suggesting that her patients' zombie-like placidity is worthy of a reward. She repeatedly misstates McMurphy's name, calling him "McMurry," as if to imply that names and other markers of individuality are unimportant and negligible. She punishes the patient Taber simply for asking what medications he is being given, and she authorizes surgery to reduce him to an unquestioning drone. Each of these deeds confirms that Nurse Ratched stands for utter compliance, self-effacement, and an almost totalitarian emphasis on fitting into a thoughtless, well-ordered world.

On the other hand, McMurphy represents the allure of personal expression, making known one's thoughts and desires, and refusing to worry about societal norms. McMurphy asserts his vitality by passing out lewd playing cards on his first day on the ward: He does not care if Ratched or the authorities are disturbed by his exuberant sense of humor and sexual energy. McMurphy breaks down the accepted barrier between Chronics and Acutes, addressing each Chronic as if he has a robust inner life and well-developed personality, refusing to see another human being as a vegetable without a soul. He ignores Bromden's status as a deaf-mute and speaks to him at length, becoming the only man in the building to notice that Bromden really can hear and comprehend other people. He laughs and sings loudly in the shower, upsetting the deadly silence of the ward, refusing to fall prey to Ratched's expectations of quiet, fearful, and self-denying behavior. His actions and attitudes demonstrate the virtues of individuality, pushing aside the urge to conform and acknowledging that every human being has eccentric wishes, thoughts, and idiosyncrasies.

Kesey suggests that the conflict between McMurphy and Ratched is a universal phenomenon by pointing out that it occurs daily within the minds of his minor characters. Harding understands the allure of conformity, accepting Ratched's cruel schedule of "analytic" sessions and trying to pin down his own freely-moving, expressive hands, but he also succumbs to McMurphy's rallying cry, muttering that Ratched is cruel and oppressive and allowing his hands to wave "beautifully" in the air. Likewise, Bromden feels torn between the desire to conform and to rebel, silencing his own voice yet admiring McMurphy and men such as his father, who turned away opportunistic government officials from his reservation when Bromden was a child. Pete suppresses most of what is going on in his head, in a way that pleases Ratched, but he also has a moment of self-expression when he attacks an orderly who has tried to pin him down. Each of these characters enacts on a private level the battle that rages between Ratched and McMurphy—the urge to comply versus the desire to be fully and unapologetically unique.

By emphasizing the conflict between nurse and free-spirited patient, Kesey thus reinforces his idea that people often fall victim to a tug-of-war between societal expectations and personal needs. Ratched demands an unquestioning acceptance of societal standards, punishing patients who challenge the daily flow of activities on her ward. By contrast, McMurphy reminds his peers that they all have personalities and inner lives, encouraging them to laugh in the face of authority whenever possible. Caught between the poles of Ratched's demands and McMurphy's free-spirited philosophy, Kesey's minor characters show how difficult it is to be oneself in a harsh, homogenous world. McMurphy's spirit rejuvenates them, but Ratched's looming presence repeatedly crushes their hopes.

LITERARY ANALYSIS

GLOSSARY OF LITERARY TERMS

ANTAGONIST

The entity that acts to frustrate the goals of the *protagonist*. The antagonist is usually another *character* but may also be a non-human force.

ANTIHERO / ANTIHEROINE

A *protagonist* who is not admirable or who challenges notions of what should be considered admirable.

CHARACTER

A person, animal, or any other thing with a personality that appears in a *narrative*.

CLIMAX

The moment of greatest intensity in a text or the major turning point in the *plot*.

CONFLICT

The central struggle that moves the *plot* forward. The conflict can be the *protagonist*'s struggle against fate, nature, society, or another person.

FIRST-PERSON POINT OF VIEW

A literary style in which the *narrator* tells the story from his or her own *point of view* and refers to himself or herself as "I." The narrator may be an active participant in the story or just an observer.

HERO / HEROINE

The principal *character* in a literary work or *narrative*.

IMAGERY

Language that brings to mind sense-impressions, representing things that can be seen, smelled, heard, tasted, or touched.

MOTIF

A recurring idea, structure, contrast, or device that develops or informs the major *themes* of a work of literature.

NARRATIVE

A story.

NARRATOR
> The person (sometimes a *character*) who tells a story; the *voice* assumed by the writer. The narrator and the author of the work of literature are not the same person.

PLOT
> The arrangement of the events in a story, including the sequence in which they are told, the relative emphasis they are given, and the causal connections between events.

POINT OF VIEW
> The *perspective* that a *narrative* takes toward the events it describes.

PROTAGONIST
> The main *character* around whom the story revolves.

SETTING
> The location of a *narrative* in time and space. Setting creates mood or atmosphere.

SUBPLOT
> A secondary *plot* that is of less importance to the overall story but may serve as a point of contrast or comparison to the main plot.

SYMBOL
> An object, *character,* figure, or color that is used to represent an abstract idea or concept. Unlike an *emblem,* a symbol may have different meanings in different contexts.

SYNTAX
> The way the words in a piece of writing are put together to form lines, phrases, or clauses; the basic structure of a piece of writing.

THEME
> A fundamental and universal idea explored in a literary work.

TONE
> The author's attitude toward the subject or *characters* of a story or poem or toward the reader.

VOICE
> An author's individual way of using language to reflect his or her own personality and attitudes. An author communicates voice through *tone, diction,* and *syntax.*

LITERARY ANALYSIS

A NOTE ON PLAGIARISM

Plagiarism—presenting someone else's work as your own—rears its ugly head in many forms. Many students know that copying text without citing it is unacceptable. But some don't realize that even if you're not quoting directly, but instead are paraphrasing or summarizing, *it is plagiarism* unless you cite the source.

Here are the most common forms of plagiarism:

- Using an author's phrases, sentences, or paragraphs without citing the source
- Paraphrasing an author's ideas without citing the source
- Passing off another student's work as your own

How do you steer clear of plagiarism? You should *always* acknowledge all words and ideas that aren't your own by using quotation marks around verbatim text or citations like footnotes and endnotes to note another writer's ideas. For more information on how to give credit when credit is due, ask your teacher for guidance or visit www.sparknotes.com.

REVIEW & RESOURCES

QUIZ

1. What physical feature does Nurse Ratched try to conceal?

   A.   Her long legs
   B.   Her blonde hair
   C.   Her large breasts
   D.   Her birthmark

2. Why did Nurse Ratched hire the three black aides?

   A.   For their strength
   B.   For their intelligence
   C.   For their stubbornness
   D.   For their hatred

3. What animals does McMurphy compare the patients to?

   A.   Wolves
   B.   Chickens
   C.   Rabbits
   D.   Pigs

4. What animals does Harding compare the patients to?

   A.   Wolves
   B.   Chickens
   C.   Rabbits
   D.   Pigs

5. What pattern covers McMurphy's boxer shorts?

   A.   White whales
   B.   Hearts
   C.   Rabbits
   D.   Kisses

6. Which character is a closeted homosexual?

    A. Nurse Ratched
    B. Billy Bibbit
    C. Dale Harding
    D. Chief Bromden

7. Which patient has been on the ward the longest?

    A. Pete Bancini
    B. Colonel Matterson
    C. Chief Bromden
    D. Maxwell Taber

8. How does Rawler, a patient on Disturbed, commit suicide?

    A. He hangs himself
    B. He drowns
    C. He cuts off his testicles
    D. He slits his throat

9. Which of the following symbolizes Bromden's insanity?

    A. The flock of geese
    B. The loud music
    C. The monopoly board
    D. The fog machine

10. What is the reward for snitching on a fellow patient?

    A. Sleeping late
    B. An extra pack of cigarettes
    C. An Accompanied Pass
    D. Skipping the Group Meeting

11. What is McMurphy's first complaint to Nurse Ratched?

    A. That the bathrooms are dirty
    B. That the music is played too loudly
    C. That he has no privacy
    D. That he cannot smoke the cigarettes he bought

12. What ailment do Sefelt and Fredrickson suffer from?

    A. Diabetes
    B. Multiple sclerosis
    C. Jaundice
    D. Epilepsy

13. Why does Doctor Spivey drive the patients and accompany them on the fishing trip?

    A. It is hospital policy to have a member of the staff accompany, and Ratched refuses to go
    B. The original driver, Sandy, does not show up
    C. Spivey is a former fisherman who insists he can show McMurphy how it is done
    D. He loses a bet to McMurphy and has no choice

14. Which character, a former seaman, captains the fishing boat?

    A. Colonel Matterson
    B. George Sorensen
    C. Doctor Spivey
    D. Dale Harding

15. What is McMurphy's excuse for breaking through the glass of the Nurses' Station?

    A. The glass was so clean he did not see it
    B. Voices in his head told him to
    C. The patients bet him he would not do it
    D. He tripped

16. What important information does the lifeguard give McMurphy?

    A. That Doctor Spivey is addicted to opiates
    B. That he was once in the NFL
    C. That committed patients can leave only at the staff's discretion
    D. That Bromden is crazy

REVIEW & RESOURCES

17. Which of Nurse Ratched's patients dies in the novel?

    A. Billy Bibbit
    B. Charles Cheswick
    C. Randle McMurphy
    D. All of the above

18. What punishment do McMurphy and Bromden receive for fighting with the aides?

    A. They have to clean the latrines
    B. They have to give up card games in the tub room
    C. They are given electroshock therapy
    D. They are given lobotomies

19. What does McMurphy do to Nurse Ratched after Billy commits suicide?

    A. He punches her in the face
    B. He rips open her shirt and strangles her
    C. He rips off her clothes and rapes her
    D. He calls her vulgar names to her face

20. Why doesn't Harding want to escape with McMurphy?

    A. He wants to leave via the correct procedures, to prove that he can
    B. He is afraid of the outside and prefers the hospital
    C. He is too drunk and he passes out
    D. He promised his wife that he would stay another year

21. How does Chief Bromden leave the hospital?

    A. He leaves with Candy and Sandy through the window
    B. He checks himself out
    C. He makes Doctor Spivey drive him away
    D. He breaks through a window and runs away

22. How does Charles Cheswick die?

    A. He falls off the boat during the fishing trip and drowns
    B. He drowns in the hospital swimming pool
    C. He receives too many electroshock treatments
    D. He has an epileptic seizure

23. What might the white whales on McMurphy's boxers symbolize?

    A. An obsessive search for evil
    B. The power of nature
    C. God
    D. All of the above

24. Which event symbolizes that Bromden is regaining his sense of self?

    A. He watches the dog outside his window
    B. He smashes the glass of the Nurse's Station
    C. He helps McMurphy win a bet by lifting the control panel
    D. He sweeps the floor during a Group Meeting

25. Who eventually kills McMurphy?

    A. Nurse Ratched
    B. McMurphy commits suicide
    C. Doctor Spivey
    D. Bromden

SUGGESTIONS FOR FURTHER READING

KAPPEL, LAWRENCE, ed. *Readings on* ONE FLEW OVER THE CUCKOO'S NEST. San Diego: Greenhaven Press, 2000.

KESEY, KEN. *Kesey's Jail Journal.* New York: Viking Adult, 2003.

LEEDS, BARRY H. *Ken Kesey.* New York: F. Ungar Publishing Co., 1981.

MCCLANAHAN, ED, ed. *Spit in the Ocean #7: All About Ken Kesey.* New York: Penguin, 2003.

PERRY, PAUL. *On the Bus: The Complete Guide to the Legendary Trip of Ken Kesey and the Merry Pranksters and the Birth of the Counterculture.* New York: Thunder's Mouth Press, 1996.

PORTER, M. GILBERT. ONE FLEW OVER THE CUCKOO'S NEST: *Rising to Heroism.* Boston: Twayne, 1989.

SAFER, ELAINE B. *The Contemporary American Comic Epic: The Novels of Barth, Pynchon, Gaddis, and Kesey.* Detroit: Wayne State University Press, 1988.

SEARLES, GEORGE J., ed. *A Casebook on Ken Kesey's* ONE FLEW OVER THE CUCKOO'S NEST. Albuquerque: University of New Mexico Press, 1992.

WHITMER, PETER O. *Aquarius Revisited: Seven Who Created the Sixties Counterculture that Changed America.* New York: Macmillan, 1987.